Jean Torshima

September 091
Bedwyn Magna

FROUDE
THE HISTORIAN
Victorian Man of Letters

FROUDE
THE HISTORIAN

Victorian Man of Letters

A.L. ROWSE

ALAN SUTTON
1987

ALAN SUTTON PUBLISHING
BRUNSWICK ROAD · GLOUCESTER

First Published 1987
Copyright © 1987 A.L. Rowse

British Library Cataloguing in Publication Data
ISBN 0–86299–384–9

Typesetting and origination by
Alan Sutton Publishing Limited
Photoset Goudy 12/14
Printed in Great Britain by
Redwood Burn Limited
Trowbridge, Wiltshire

To
Hugh Trevor-Roper
a successor to Froude
as Regius Professor of Modern History
at Oxford

Contents

Characteristics

Froude is the last of the great Victorian writers to be resuscitated and placed in his proper place among them. It is odd that this has not been done before. In the Victorian age he was the only historian to compare with Macaulay in achievement, force and style as a writer, and in the response of the public to his work. His books sold in hundreds of thousands; he was read all over the English-speaking world; he was a public figure. Why the contrast in their respective fortunes and fame today?

Macaulay was a fortunate man, as Leslie Stephen says, and had all the luck. He was the foremost exponent of the Whig interpretation of history, with its over-estimation of the rôle of Parliament, which – except for Hume – held the field up to our own, more *désabusé*, time. He was in the centre of the Parliamentary tradition; he trumpeted the Victorian belief in progress, in a plain and straightforward manner, for he was a plain and straightforward man with no doubts. He had the dominant school of thought with him, and a family of gifted historians, the Trevelyans, to carry on his work and speak up for him. And there is a veritable Cambridge cult of him to this day.

James Anthony Froude (1818–1894) had none of these advantages. He was not a Whig; he had no very

high opinion of Parliament or parliamentary politic-
ians. He was not in the mainstream; he was entirely
independent, and had no school of followers. Though
his standards were academic, he was constantly attacked by academic critics, mainly from Oxford, his own
university, which indeed treated him badly. Yet the
leader of the Oxford school, Bishop Stubbs, admitted
in the end: 'Froude was a man of genius, and he has
been treated abominably.'

Why?

To some extent the reaction to his work is understandable. Froude did not so much fall between two
stools, as among them all. Brought up in the heart of
the Oxford Movement – his brilliant brother Hurrell
being Newman's right hand (and more) until his early
death – Anthony Froude became the fugleman of the
English Reformation, which the High Church party
detested. Though his historic sympathies were Protestant, and even Calvinist, he could not be much
appreciated by them; for, underneath his moralism
and preaching up Protestant backbone, his temperament was sceptical; he had no use for doctrine and was
not really a Christian believer. This was awkward for a
Victorian.

Beginning as a radical – much in sympathy with his
brother-in-law, Charles Kingsley (who was also disapproved of for his Chartist sympathies) – Froude
became a prophet of Empire, though a highly critical
one, of its record in Ireland, South Africa and the
West Indies. He was an admirer of British rule in
India, an unsurpassed record in history. Of the two
outstanding figures who dominated, and polarised, the
late Victorian scene, Gladstone and Disraeli, Froude

was critical: he disliked the humbug of the former, and suspected charlatanism in the latter, admiring the writer in Disraeli rather than the politician. Indeed Froude had little opinion of party-politicians, and no humbug – a defect in the Victorian world. Though a famous figure in society, he was regarded as 'enigmatic' – even by Leslie Stephen, who knew him well (they were both deacons in the Church and threw off their orders to become laymen). People could not quite make Froude out. This too was understandable: ordinary people do not understand genius, and Froude was a complicated man, not all on the surface.

Most of the subjects he wrote about were controversial. The subject of his grand History, from the Reformation Parliament to the Spanish Armada, the conflict between Catholicism and Protestantism, was a living issue in the 19th century, and the leading characters in the drama were all subjects of dispute. He wrote much about Ireland, including one large-scale work, *The English in Ireland*, from the Civil War to the Act of Union in 1801. Everything about Ireland is controverted, and Froude did not mince his opinions about anything. It is quite all right to attack the English: they don't mind; but one mustn't reflect on the Irish. Froude spoke out on both sides; when he lectured on the subject in America – he was a brave man to do so – even his life was threatened.

In writing about South Africa and the West Indies, Froude spoke his mind on race relations and the colour question. Here he held the old-fashioned views of a century ago: he did not think that blacks

3

were better than whites – very un-modern of him; he held rather the contrary. A life-long friend of Carlyle, he wrote one of the finest of English literary biographies on this outsize figure. Every one of Froude's books raised controversy, but this one raged most fiercely of all, strange to say. He was taken aback by the uncalled-for outburst, which embittered and overclouded his last years. There are circumstances to account for it – and yet there is something inexplicable in the antagonism Froude aroused, even apart from the fact that he challenged so many people's prejudices.

What was it in him that provoked? I have come across this antagonism to him in academics even today. Of course he stated his views uncompromisingly, and he did not trouble to explain or defend himself. Evidently he thought that his work spoke for itself. But this is never enough, humans being what they are.

We may find some part of the explanation by considering his work, though here we must concentrate on the historian. Actually he was an all-round man who touched Victorian life on many sides and wrote prolifically. He contributed important, long essays to a number of periodicals, and for many years edited a leading one, *Fraser's*. During two decades he gave the best of his mind to the great History. He wrote a couple of early novels – *Shadows of the Clouds* and *The Nemesis of Faith* – which created scandal among the faithful; the Sub-Rector of Exeter College threw the latter on the fire in the hall, while his father, Archdeacon Froude, bought up copies to suppress it. A later historical novel, *The Two Chiefs of*

Dunboy,[1] revealed 'his appreciation of the Irish scene and his intimate knowledge of Irish character and ways.

He took a hand in politics, when his friend, Lord Caernarvon,[2] sent him out to South Africa to report on prospects of confederation. This was premature, and led to more controversy; it does not seem that Froude was wrong in his prognostications, but this was another case – like Ireland – where the circle could not be squared. Nor has it been. There are some situations in men's affairs which cannot be got right. Froude travelled round the world on his own mission of Imperial Federation, though sceptical whether it could ever come about – meanwhile scattering pages of vivid descriptions of the landscapes then unspoiled, like the marvellous Pink and White Terraces of Rotorua in New Zealand. One of these travel-books, *The English in the West Indies*, he illustrated with his own sketches from on the spot.

He was exceptionally talented, with a good hand at handling a boat. Sailing was his passion, and this illuminates his many writings about the sea, from his famous essay, 'England's Forgotten Worthies', which

1. I regard this vivid and exciting story, with its portrayal of the early 18th century conflict in Ireland, but too long in the original, well worth reviving, and published a shortened version of it in 1969 (Chatto and Windus).
2. Froude's letters have never been collected, though many are quoted in W.H. Dunn, *James Anthony Froude: A Biography*. Oxford, 1961. I recommend their pursuit and publication to the indefatigable American editors of less rewarding letter-writers. Letters to Caernarvon should be at Highclere, those to Lady Derby at Knowsley, to the Salisburys at Hatfield, etc.

inspired Kingsley's *Westward Ho*, onwards. He told Tennyson that the most necessary gift for a historian was imagination. Tennyson responded by writing his ballad of the *Revenge*, inspired by Froude's account of Grenville's heroic action at the Azores, and basing his play 'Queen Mary' on that volume in the History. The historian was an equally skilled fisherman – hence the nostalgic essays on the fiords of Norway, and 'A Fortnight in Kerry'.

At Salcombe he kept his sailing boat. A rather silent man normally, he one day broke silence there to a youth, who became an old acquaintance of mine: 'What do you think enables me to keep this boat, and a man to look after it all the year round? – the American royalties on the first volume of *Short Studies on Great Subjects*.' His literary success and his social eminence did not endear him to his academic critics. He was welcomed in the great world: a friend of the Lansdownes, Derbys and Salisburys, of the Colonial Secretary Lord Caernarvon; Lord Elphinstone accompanied him in South Africa and Australia, and contributed the sketches that illustrate *Oceana*, most delightful of his travel books.

For all his fame and his friends, Froude was essentially a solitary man. Few there were who really knew him; in society he was thought to be rather cynical, for he had no illusions. He seems to have had little sense of humour, unlike Macaulay's rollicking sense of fun – everybody knew *him*. The truth was that Anthony Froude was a deeply wounded man; he did not choose to show his inner face to the world, and he never complained. His youth was unhappy; he was brutally beaten at his school, Westminster, and at home. His mother, a Spedding, died young, and 'the suppression of sentiment so sternly insisted upon among us prevented my father from ever mentioning her'. His father, Archdeacon of Totnes, was a Tory parson-squire of the old school, unsympathetic to the unpromising ugly duckling of the family – who grew up into a notably handsome man, with striking lambent eyes.

The mother had introduced consumption into the brood. Three brothers died of it – there is the family grave beside the old ruined church at lovely Dartington in Devon. One of Froude's own daughters died young of it. He did not find himself until he was a man of thirty, and looked back upon those early years with disapproval and remorse. His first marriage – to a Cornish Grenfell, sister to Kingsley's wife – was not happy; she died early, of drug addiction.[1] The son of this marriage was a ne'er-do-well, never mentioned, who died young, a remittance-man in South Africa. Froude's second marriage was entirely happy, but the wife died years before him, leaving him disconsolate and lonelier than ever – save for the remaining daughter, the highly intelligent Margaret Froude.

There was genius in the family. The eldest brother, Hurrell, 1803–36 was touched with it – and would have made a name along with Newman and Manning if he had lived. As it was, the publication of his *Remains* made a sensation, and something of a scandal for its revelation of the inner, rather homo-erotic feelings in the Newman circle.[2] He had been a

1. From family information.
2. cf. Geoffrey Faber, *Oxford Apostles*.

somewhat brutal inquisitor to the youthful Anthony, who, however, admired him for the remarkable man he was. Another brother, William Froude 1810–79, was a genius as a naval engineer; his life's work in studying, experimenting and correcting the rolling of ships at sea was of the highest importance. After decades of resistance from a complacent Admiralty, Froude conducted his experiments and developed his inventions at his own expense, contributing greatly to the seaworthiness of all ships, particularly those of the Queen's Navy. I am afraid that I am incapable of understanding 'Froude's Law', which he contributed to naval science. He received no reward for his life's work, any more than his brother received any public recognition for his. And now, so far as I am aware, this brilliant family is at an end, with the historian's only grandson killed in the first German war, 1914–1918.

We must confine ourselves to the historian, and ask what were his qualifications, the particular gifts he brought to the job, and what his defects?

Even his enemies – and he had many – always admitted his genius. Difficult to define with precision, it meant that he was possessed by a driving spirit of his own, by an exceptional force in his way of looking at things, and he had the inspiration to impress his personality on everything that he wrote. Again everyone admitted the magic of his style, as remarkable as Macaulay's, more flexible and varied, less rhetorical and even more poetic. Famous passages are quoted among the best specimens of English prose in anthologies – something exceptional for an historian. But, then, Froude was no ordinary historian.

The best known passage is that in which he evoked, in the first chapter of his History, the transition from the medieval to the modern world wrought by the Reformation, which was his subject. Here he was evoking the *spirit* of the change – he would bring to light a multitude of facts to bring it down to earth in the course of the work.

'For, indeed, a change was coming upon the world . . . a change from era to era. The paths trodden by the footsteps of ages were broken up; old things were passing away; the faith and the life of ten centuries were dissolving like a dream. Chivalry was dying; the abbey and the castle were soon together to crumble into ruins; and all the forms, desires, beliefs, convictions of the old world were passing away, never to return. A new continent had risen up beyond the western sea. The floor of heaven, inlaid with stars, had sunk back into an infinite abyss of immeasurable space; and the firm earth itself, unfixed from its foundations, was seen to be but a small atom in the awful vastness of the universe. In the fabric of habit which they had so laboriously built for themselves, mankind were to remain no longer.

And now it is all gone – like an unsubstantial pageant faded; and between us and the old English there lies a gulf of mystery which the prose of the historian will never adequately bridge. They cannot come to us, and our imagination can but feebly penetrate to them. Only among the aisles of the cathedral, only as we gaze upon their silent figures sleeping on their tombs, some faint conceptions float before us of what these men were when they were alive; and perhaps in the sound of church bells, that peculiar creation of medieval age, which falls upon the ear like the echo of a vanished world.'

Not exact in every detail: for example, the clang of medieval church bells was different from the beautiful change-ringing, the peculiar creation of 18th century England. What matter? Froude showed that he had sympathy with the strangeness of the medieval world to a modern mind. This he expressed in a number of notable essays. More important, Froude catches the mystery of the medieval mind, the profound difficulty of reaching into it, with its different codes and values, cocooned within the bounds of faith – broken as it was in the 16th century, when the modern mind, as Froude saw it, was liberated.

His sceptical bent was such that he doubted whether we could arrive at objective fact – only at the facts as handed down to us by other minds at other times. Unlike Macaulay, Froude did not wholly eschew speculative thought, which appears in several of his essays – the famous one on the Book of Job, for example, or 'A Plea for the Free Discussion of Theological Difficulties.' He was better educated: he had read not only Hume, but Goethe and – more surprisingly – Schopenhauer. But he relegated philosophical speculation to a secondary place. He thought that the inner *truth* of men's minds was more convincingly revealed by Shakespeare, a better guide to it and thus a better historian. Curiously enough, the most academic of contemporary Oxford historians, K.B. McFarlane, wrote that Shakespeare was the best historian of us all.

Thus Froude was primarily interested in the drama of events and historic personalities. An Oxford critic, J.R. Green, said that Froude's work was history 'with the people left out'. This was not so: his much-admired first chapter, on the 'Social Condition of England', had the favoured modern approach to their general circumstances, expectations and conditions of life, wages and prices all set out. And at intervals throughout, he deals with the people when they emerge into historical significance and make themselves heard, with such events as the Pilgrimage of Grace or the Rebellions of 1549 and 1569, treating them with more consideration than is warranted. For what good did these do?

Froude accepted, as we must accept, the primacy of political history; for it is upon the political plane that societies project themselves most conspicuously and concentratedly, and where the decisions are made. He realised well enough that the impulse towards Reformation came up from below, but what was characteristic of it in England was that the revolution was led from on top. Thus the importance he gave to the Statute Book and the lengthy preambles to Acts of Parliament; for these explained and defended the purpose of the revolutionary legislation carried through – in this sense they were also propaganda. For the revolution carried out by Henry VIII – the breach with Rome, the subordination of the Church to the State, the achievement of a modern secular state, etc – was conducted at every stage with the consensus of the bulk of the governing class represented in Parliament. If it had not been, it could never have been carried through at all.

To his task, conceived on the grand scale, Froude brought immense industry; he was a tireless worker, and we must pay tribute to him as the first of historical researchers in the modern archival sense. Even Macaulay depended more on printed material, and the public was more aware of the 17th century than it was informed about the 16th. Froude devoted himself to the archives, like a Ranke: at home, the Record Office, British Museum, Bodleian, Westminster Abbey, Hatfield House; abroad, the Spanish archives at Simancas, where he was first in the field, in Paris, Brussels, Vienna. He got proper credit even from people who disagreed, though little qualified, with his conclusions for the vast amount of new information he thus brought to light – notably about the controversial character of Henry VIII, the conservative revolutionary who, like a Stalin, forced through the revolution. Henry's real political achievement, apart from his personality with his obvious 'personality defects' – to use a contemporary cliché, familiar enough in Russia – was little understood before Froude.

On the more technical side we should consider his visual gift, for describing landscape and scene: such dramatic events as the Pilgrimage of Grace or the reception of Cardinal Pole (when poor Mary Tudor thought she felt the babe leap in her womb: *Benedictus fructus tui ventris*, said the Cardinal under equal hallucination); the arrival of the Spanish Armada on the coast, or the execution of Mary Queen of Scots – so vividly described that it made the warm-hearted Carlyle 'shudder'.

What then are Froude's defects?

We must distinguish, so far as we can, between those owing to the Victorian Age, the mental atmosphere of the time in which he lived, and those special to Froude though to some extent they run into each

other. The dominant feature of the age was its moral
earnestness. To be just, this was a factor urging
forward its tremendous achievement. But things, and
people, have the defects of their qualities. All the
great Victorian writers were damaged by excessive
moralism – Dickens, Thackeray, Ruskin, while
George Eliot was rendered a bore by it. At its most
conspicuous it became sheer humbug – of which
Gladstone was a shining exemplar, while George
Eliot, for all her high-mindedness – 'O may I join the
choir invisible' – lived in sin with George Henry
Lewes. Yet people would touch the hem of her garment
as she swept by into a concert! Froude had no humbug;
but his excessive moralism was re-inforced by the
intolerable influence of Carlyle, so strong with Victorians: one can hear the style re-echoed in both
Dickens and Ruskin. Thank goodness Froude was not
in the least influenced by Carlyle's unbearable style –
he had a better model in Newman. Again we must
distinguish between the History and the Essays, where
the preachy–preachy element is to us displeasing, if
understandable when the subject is topical.

A great deal in Froude was topical, and still is. He
was aroused to the defence of the Reformation by its
denigration by the Oxford Movement. His life-long
concern with Ireland arose from the fact that Ireland
was a foremost concern of politics throughout the 19th
century, and – alas – is still topical.

This raises in its most acute form the question of
bias, for which Froude has been chiefly criticised. But
all historians have their bias. Gibbon was notoriously
biased against Christianity, and gave no credit to the
early medieval Church for its grandest work, the

civilisation of the Northern barbarians. Froude was not biased against medieval Catholicism, though he rejected its miracles and superstitions. He was hostile to the Counter-Reformation, with its interference in European politics and in the internal affairs in secular states, as in Elizabethan England – as with so notorious a politico as the Jesuit Parsons.[1] On the other hand Froude paid tribute to the good work of the Jesuits in the West Indies.

Summary judgments, all too easily dismissive, are to be deplored whether in history or literature – people and things are often too complex, and there is usually something to be said on both sides of the question. Actually Froude was fair to both the great Emperor Charles V and to the lesser, if over-burdened Philip II. He was just to the latter's sincere attempt at compromise in the Netherlands, before it was ruined by Don Juan – far more so than the simple-minded Motley, who could see only the Protestant side of the case. Froude regarded this kind of view of Charles V and Philip as mere 'Protestant caricatures'.

He worked far too fast and wrote too much, with no secretarial help, except for some aid from a brother-in-law with the Spanish archives. Anyone who is acquainted with 16th century hands will know how difficult some of them are to decipher, sometimes practically impossible to make out for certain. Froude went through some hundreds of volumes of papers at Simancas alone, in that beautifully panelled and ordered cabinet-room Philip had constructed, but the

1. cf. my account of him in *Eminent Elizabethans*.

latter wrote one of the most difficult hands to decipher on record.

So Froude was apt to make mistakes of detail – not that these were important in themselves; nor did he respect 'the sanctity of inverted commas.' I came across a couple of such mistakes in *The English in the West Indies*, which could easily have been avoided, if only he had had an assistant to check things for him. He was essentially thrown on his own – and, as every writer knows, especially in the decline of standards today, there are always misprints created for one. The irascible Freeman, Regius Professor at Oxford, made a great song and dance about Froude's inaccuracies, and conducted a campaign for some twenty years against every couple of volumes that came out at intervals. Freeman had a personal hatred of Froude, who for the most part ignored him. It was also an intellectual vendetta: Freeman was a High Church academic, a Liberal follower of Gladstone; Froude, though reared by the High Churchmen, turned his back on the Oxford Movement to become the foremost defender of the Reformation, and was an Erastian with a secular outlook, with no use for religious dogma or Mr Gladstone.

On the technical side, the academic Freeman never went beyond printed sources in his voluminous History of the Norman Conquest; Froude, the man of the world, spent months, indeed years, all told, in the archives working at original materials. In his day most of the State Papers were as yet unpublished, and Froude was careful to place his transcripts from the archives in the Record Office for others to consult. When Martin Hume came to edit the Spanish State

Papers he found that Froude's transcripts were essentially reliable, inverted commas or no.

More important than these technical details is the question of interpretation. Practically all the 19th century historians were Teutonic fanciers, over-emphasising the Anglo-Saxon elements in the make-up of the English people, even if dominant, and under-stating, not troubling to understand, the Celtic, or even the Roman, elements in the formation of a richer, more complex and variegated Britain. Perhaps this was to be expected from persons with such names as Freeman and Green and Stubbs. Here Froude was no exception; he too was a Teutonist, though not to the absurd extent of his brother-in-law Kingsley, with his cult of the 'North-Easter'. As for Freeman, he idealised the Anglo-Saxons, and could not forgive the Norman Conquest; in the semi-Dane, rather barbaric Earl Godwin, father of Harold 'Last of the Saxons', he saw a kind of 11th century Gladstone.

Freeman got his comeuppance from J.H. Round; then Round got his comeuppance from Maitland, who also gave the great Stubbs his comeuppance over the supposed independence of the medieval Church in England from Rome. Now we learn that the sainted Maitland – ideal of modern historical technicians – has received his comeuppance from Samuel Thorne. Most of his work on *Domesday Book and Beyond*, and on the development of the Common Law in the Middle Ages, has been superseded: 'of all this very little now stands'.[1] Practically the whole of Stubb's big *Constitutional History* has been put out of court;

1. G.R. Elton, *F.W. Maitland*, 43.

nobody now accepts his theory of Lancastrian constit-
utionalism, any more than of the independence of the
Church in medieval England. So what?

Well, the documents remain. So, too, does history
as art. So, too, do facts, if we can establish them. The
great physiologist, Sherrington, tells us that a fact is
not superseded. All three are the business of the
historian, and it is otiose to exclude one or the other.
Seeley's famous declaration, which so angered the
young Trevelyan at Cambridge, that 'history is a
science, no more and no less', is seen to be silly. I
conclude, in the light of all this, that it is best for the
historian to be sparing of theory and theorising; a little
is enough, more is liable to lead him astray – as with
the sociological structures which have been so fashionable in this century, now visibly crumbling in their
turn. Better to stick to facts, elicit the truth of the
story, and tell it with the aid of common sense, what
we know from experience and our knowledge of
human nature – and with imaginative understanding,
if we have it. Froude had it to an exceptional degree.

How does his work stand up in the light of this? It is
difficult for the ordinary reader to appreciate how
much of it does in fact stand up, simply because so
much of it has been absorbed into our present understanding of Tudor England. Before Froude's work it
was largely incomprehended. It appears to me that the
lines laid down in his History are not essentially
departed from by modern Tudor historians. There are
differences of opinion, of course, differing judgments
of character and person according to taste, particularly
according to sectarian partisanship. Froude himself
wrote that, if a man is a Catholic, one can predict that

he will present a Catholic view of events; if a Protestant, then a Protestant view.

We should today be above this limitation. And for a profound reason that the ordinary person should not find it impossible to grasp. So much of what happens in human affairs, in politics, in history, is unavoidable, if not inevitable. This should obviate the littleness of taking sides in accordance with prejudice, or even sentiment. The Reformation was like a geological fault, the breaking away of most of Northern Europe from the age-long ascendancy of the Mediterranean and Rome, so long the centre of the civilised world.

Perhaps I may conclude with my own personal counts against Froude. I do not like his rhetoric or his summary judgments – but those are characteristic of the age. I dislike his exaggerations of phrase. Though in personal and social life he was courteous and gallant to women, in his History he seems to me unappreciative and even unfair to them. He was very much a manly man; 'manly' was a favourite commendation with him. I find this a limitation. He could do more than justice to such masculine types as Henry VIII or Luther, Latimer or rebarbative John Knox; but he detested Mary Queen of Scots. It is true that she was a murderess of her husband; but – as a Catholic historian, Archbishop David Mathew, once said sagely to me, 'nobody brought up at the Court of the Valois would find the idea of assassination at all remote'. Strangely, in my view, Froude did grave injustice to Anne Boleyn, and even more to her daughter, Elizabeth I. Perhaps they were, apart from anything else, just too feminine.

My gravest charge is that he was no aesthete. But

then, among historians, who is? Froude thought morals more important than things of beauty. I do not. Human beings are what they are: no historian should have any illusions about them. 'Things and actions are what they are, and the consequences of them will be what they will be: why then should we desire to be deceived?', wrote the philosophic Bishop Butler. In my view only works of art and intellect redeem mankind from the slime; only they remain, the creations of elect spirits, when ordinary humans recur and are forgotten. The only historian of the 19th century who understood this was the historian of the Italian Renaissance, Burckhardt. Him Froude had not read, nor would he have appreciated his gospel if he had.

Henry VIII's Reformation

Froude's first venture in historical writing had its comic side, though not without a certain symbolism for the future. Newman was piloting a propaganda series of Lives of the English Saints, and gave the neophyte – who had occupied the rooms above his own in Oriel – the job of contributing the Life of St Neot. After having written enough of the infantile miracles and superstitions about the saint, young Anthony concluded, 'This is all, and indeed rather more than all, that is known of the blessed St Neot.' To this a wag added, 'But not more than is known to the angels in heaven'.

The interesting thing is that Froude was never touched by the mythology of the Oxford Movement to which he was so close, and was never credulous. Nevertheless he always retained respect for Newman, in spite of his credulity and his apostasy from the English Church. (Several members of the Froude family followed him to Rome.) Newman used the exceptional finesse of his intellect – 'Oriel Common Room stank of logic' – to insist how slender are the grounds on which we know anything outside ourselves: so, why not angels? why not the liquefaction of the blood of St Januarius? He was willing to accept a great deal of nonsense. In later life he wrote a remarkable book, *The Grammar of Assent*, which for all the difficulty of its argument, Froude was not afraid to tackle, and treat respectfully in one of the Short Studies.

His early Oxford career was cut short by the scandal of *The Nemesis of Faith* and the resignation of his Fellowship at Exeter. What was he to do? There were no openings for an unbelieving young deacon, and he thought of emigrating – as similar fellows afflicted with disbelief were doing, Arthur Clough, Tom Arnold, Samuel Butler. Froude contemplated Tasmania, as he recalled when he visited it years later. He was saved from this fate by a visit to Kingsley at Bideford, where he fell for the sister-in-law, and both sisters, being Grenfells, had private means.

He began his literary career by writing essays, of substantial length in those days, for a number of periodicals: the *Fortnightly*, *Fraser's*, the *Oxford and Cambridge Review*, the *Eclectic* (appropriate for one in his position), above all for the *Westminster Review*, then the most distinguished organ of intellectual Radicalism. Its gospel was Benthamite Utilitarianism, which no more fitted Froude's outlook than the *Edinburgh Review* did Carlyle, with which *he* began.

The underlying bent of Froude's mind was sceptical, and, without the prop of faith, he went through the intellectual crisis which upheaved a number of the most sensitive minds of his generation – George Eliot, for one, a fellow-contributor with whom he corresponded. He was reduced to something like despair, until he met Carlyle – who was capable of giving a positive charge of energy, 'The Everlasting Yea', to anyone, except apparently his wife.

It is usual to describe Froude as Carlyle's 'disciple'; it would be more accurate to describe Carlyle as Froude's mentor. He developed an intellectual position of his own; nor was he taken in by Carlyle's dismissive estimates of his contemporaries: Newman having the 'intellect of a rabbit', for example; Carlyle had more original genius, but he had nothing of Newman's intellectual subtlety or logical equipment. Froude respected both – the two poles of the *Zeitgeist* to him.

We should say, rather, that Carlyle reinforced tendencies that were already there: the original Protestant inflexion of Froude's upbringing. The respect he had for the Reformation, as a liberation from the shackles of Catholicism, informed the History he now contemplated writing which was in part a reaction to continual detraction by the Oxford Movement, and Catholic historians like Lingard. Froude probably derived the harsh strain of Calvinism, along with his over-estimation of the shrill Knox, from Carlyle. Carlyle also emphasised the role of force and action in men's affairs, the doers as against the talkers – he himself was a mere talker, as Mrs Carlyle pointed out to Mazzini. This emphasis led to the lack of esteem by both Froude and Carlyle for political parties and Parliament.

Here an important point must be made in regard to historiography. Today historians realise that the central spine of English history is *not* constituted by Parliament, as Victorian historians would have it. The backbone of our constitutional history is the Crown and Council, in changing, evolutionary development: in other words, the executive, government itself. In this regard Hume was nearer the truth than the Whig historians. Froude's view of the 16th century was, also, again closer to the fact of the matter than, say, a liberal Parliamentarian like A.F. Pollard or his pupil, Neale. Froude was not mesmerised by Parliament. The English Reformation was led, and carried through, by the sovereign and his advisers, notably Thomas Cromwell; Parliament was called into consultation and, by an indubitable majority supported the new deal.

One more specialised point: most English people fail to realise what a different country Scotland has been, with a differing social structure and historical tradition, a mind of its own and a religious outlook in Calvinist Presbyterianism quite uncongenial to the English mind. Froude understood it, partly through Carlyle, but, in later years, more discriminatingly through his close friendship with John Skelton.[1] (In his *Table Talk of Shirley* we get our best close-up of the charming man Froude was in private; in public, after all he had had to put up with, he was reserved, with a rather *désabusé* carapace.) This in part accounts for his over-favourable attitude to Calvinism. He devoted a Short Study to the subject, 'The Influence of the Reformation on the Scottish Character', and an Address on Calvinism, when he was elected Lord Rector of St Andrew's University, directed against Disraeli. On the one hand it means that his History is better informed on Scottish affairs than is usual with English historians. On the other hand, his view is

---

1. The leading Scottish historian, Hume Brown, told the historian Grant Robertson that Froude was the only English historian who understood the history of Scotland during the Reformation.

heavily biased against Mary Queen of Scots in favour of her politic half-brother, the Regent Moray (it is true that she pensioned his murderer). Today we should prefer the point of view of a real *politique*, like Maitland of Lethington, clever man, but defeated by the fanatics.

Froude originally intended to write the story of Elizabeth I's reign, but found that the foundation of the achievement of the Elizabethan Age was the Henrician Reformation, and that he would have to begin with that. He showed the proofs of the first two volumes to Carlyle. Anyone who has seen the marginal comments of the older and more experienced writer will be struck by the shrewdness and practicality of the advice Carlyle gave.[1] One cannot go into detail, but its tendency was in favour of tightening up the narrative: Froude would have done well to heed that more. Useful practical points occur, such as keeping to English in the text, quotations in foreign languages in the footnotes. Carlyle has been blamed for encouraging Froude to make a Hero of Henry VIII – in accord with Carlyle's naif gospel of Hero-worship. I do not think that this was so: Froude had his own view of the 'majestic lord that broke the bonds of Rome', and his own reasons for admiring the historic achievement. We shall see how it developed.

---

1. Margaret Froude gave these proofs, with other materials to Waldo H. Dunn, who was to write the official biography. He took the whole *Nachlass* to Wooster College, Ohio, where I inspected it. His intention was to bequeath this material to Yale University. Some impression of it may be gathered from Herbert Paul's *Life of Froude*, 80 foll.

Whatever we may think of Henry VIII (he is not my cup of tea: I prefer his father), he is one of the decisive figures in English history, as was his right-hand man in the revolution, Thomas Cromwell (again, not my fancy: I prefer Thomas More). An historian must set aside his personal preferences and aim at justice in his judgments, making an intellectual effort as against emotional or sentimental feeling. Few writers, especially reviewers, seem capable of justice of mind, rarest of qualities: they simply follow their prejudices, so common, and so boring to the judicious.

In considering a controversial figure like Henry VIII we should make a distinction between the personal and the political. As a man, he was an absorbed male egoist, capricious and cruel, though he could be considerate also, and exert commanding charm. He was an able politician, more able as such than Cromwell and that was his job, to keep the command in society, no easy job in time of revolution. The clue to him personally is that he turned after his Yorkist grandfather, Edward IV: a big man, handsome when young, oversize when older, running to fat; an out-of-doors man, of considerable gifts, ambitious to shine in the field, and above all, a man of action.

Before Froude everybody had judged Henry VIII in personal terms: he was a 'tyrant', a 'despot', etc. He was neither a tyrant, nor a despot in the precise meaning of those terms: people never know the correct use of them, any more than the proper meaning of the word 'arrogant'. Henry was an autocrat and he had a tigerish pounce, just like the Yorkists, who practically finished off the Lancastrian Royal house and then killed off each other. Henry followed suit in killing off his Yorkist cousins, the Marquis of Exeter and, shockingly, the aged, but undaunted, Countess of Salisbury, Clarence's daughter. Not a town-cat mewed when he executed these aristocrats; like his grandfather, Edward IV, Henry always remained popular. Froude pointed that out, and the significance of that popularity.

Froude decided to do what had not been done before, to take the Statute Book and the State Papers as his guide. This had an enormous advantage for estimating Henry's political achievement; it also had a secondary disadvantage: Froude was apt to take not only the government's point of view but its statement of the case.

Take the crucial case of Anne Boleyn, or consider the execution of Cromwell, or for that matter of More and Fisher. We must consider each case on its merits, or demerits; we must discriminate. Froude pointed out that Henry's marriage to Anne Boleyn was essentially a political act, or he would not have waited so long as he did or gone through the prolonged agony of the divorce proceedings from Catherine. There had always been doubt about the validity of that marriage anyway. The very first month of Anne's pregnancy Henry married her, secretly, in January 1533, in the expectation that the child of love would be the longed-for, and indeed utterly demanded (by everybody) son and heir.

Anne's first failure was to produce a daughter, Elizabeth, that September. Her second, and fatal, failure was to produce no more children, but to miscarry of a still-born son in January 1536. Henry waited, month by month. By now he had turned against Anne, who was not a nice woman, had behaved badly to Queen Catherine and her daughter, and had never loved him anyway. He was not going to go through the anguish of waiting for a son for years again; in a sense he could not afford to, he actually explained his predicament publicly. He had been too patient, for at his death he left a boy of only nine to succeed him and how the rapacious lot who governed for him played fast and loose with the country's interests, grasping all they could while they had the chance! Only a firm hand could guide the country through the revolution and Henry certainly had that.

In May 1536 he struck, to get rid of Anne, and solve his problem. Cromwell had to do the dirty work and mount the case against the poor woman. Anne had levity, not regal dignity, and allowed liberties in the little circle around her – which was entirely pro-French in its sympathies, as was Anne (she had been brought up in the fast atmosphere of the Valois Court). The country, and Henry himself, wanted the restoration of good relations with the Emperor Charles V; trade demanded it. Catherine of Aragon having died, this was now possible. The bitter irony of Anne's position was that now a clearance could be made, and Henry could make an indubitably legitimate marriage, which would produce an indubitably legitimate son and heir – as it did, in young Edward.

This is the politics behind the events, and people can judge persons, rather than politics. Anne had no party behind her, and no support; Cromwell slipped over to the other side to do the necessary, and fabricated the case against her with his usual efficiency or even more so, for the 'evidence' against her, incest with her brother, etc, is quite incredible. Every one of her intimates who was charged asserted his innocence, except the lower-class musician who 'confessed' – no doubt he was promised his life to do so, and then got rid of. (We have been made familiar with the technique in our time, with Stalin.) The Emperor Charles V's sister, who was governing in the Netherlands and understood the ways of high politics, wrote: 'Only the little organist confessed: they wanted to get rid of her'.

Everybody wanted to get rid of her: it was a political necessity. She was, in familiar modern terms, 'framed', and her disappearance was quite acceptable. Henry at once married Jane Seymour; she did her duty in conceiving a son, at last. The conservatives, the Lady Mary and Lady Salisbury came back to Court to attend on the indubitably legitimate Queen, the wife with whom Henry chose to be buried at Windsor, in assertion of the fact. Elizabeth I knew how shamelessly her mother had been treated, though she could never utter a word against her father the King; when she became Queen she showed what she thought, silently, by going out of her way to be good to the children of those who had died for her mother.

The relevance of all this is that Froude accepted the government's statement of the case. In spite of his own Protestant sympathies – and to Protestant opinion Anne was a martyr – Froude felt that he could not go against the formidable indictment built up against her and accepted by the court of peers who sat in judgment upon her. Well, we know better today how they managed these things in Stalin's Russia.

Similarly with the execution of Cromwell: Froude accepted the case against him – again surprisingly, if one considers Froude as simply pro-Protestant. There *was* a case against Cromwell. In the critical circumstances of 1539–40, when Henry feared a combination of both France and the Empire against England, Cromwell forced his hand, impelled him into an alliance with the Protestants in Germany, sealing it with the marriage to Anne of Cleves. Here was a gamble indeed! So long as the crisis continued and danger threatened, Henry held to it. The moment Charles and Francis fell out and the danger had passed, Henry put the unappetising 'Flanders mare' away – on generous terms. (Anne of Cleves enjoyed the rest of her life in England.)

Cromwell had chanced his hand too far, and committed Henry not only beyond his wishes, but beyond what proved politically necessary. Cromwell had no friends, (except Cranmer, ineffectually, no party behind him, no support except Henry's, and universal hostility. Henry wavered for a time; but, after all, his judgment of the international situation had proved better than Cromwell's: he could be dispensed with. His execution was, once more, a popular political act. Personally, a little later, Henry expressed regret at missing the service of his ablest minister, and he recompensed Cromwell's son by promoting him to the peerage.

Perhaps I may be permitted a merely personal opinion here. Cromwell carried to the convenient grave Henry's most compromising secret, that about Anne Boleyn. And I regard the executions of Anne and Cromwell, those pre-eminent figures of the new deal, as Henry's most unforgivable acts. Here I differ from Froude. I do not regard the executions of More and Fisher in the same light. Again we must discriminate. Bishop Fisher was a traitor: he was in correspondence with the enemy, Emperor and Pope, to bring about the invasion of his country. Sir Thomas More was not a traitor; but he stood out before European opinion as the most eminent Englishman in opposition to what was not merely Henry's personal policy but that agreed upon by the great majority of the country, in state and Church, by Parliament and all the bishops (except Fisher). It was reported that Anne Boleyn drove Henry on against More. What is clear is that the King felt a sense of personal betrayal in the opposition, in his dire need, of the man whom he had delighted to honour. Everybody else agreed, so why not More? In the event Henry's urgent course proved successful, and More, from a secular point of view, wrong. The commonsense of the historian cannot answer for the angels in heaven.

Let us take Froude's treatment of the Dissolution of the Monasteries as a test of his historical writing. It comes early in his career, in the second volume of the History which was ultimately to contain twelve. As a Victorian moralist Froude emphasises the sexual misconduct of the monks, where we should think in economic and social terms, and (for myself) aesthetic. No doubt the Visitation of the monasteries over-emphasised the laxity and shortcomings of the monks. But there is no doubt that they had largely lost their earlier sense of vocation, and should mostly, not necessarily all, have been reformed out of existence. Cardinal Wolsey had set the pattern, with his suppression of some twenty-six small houses of monks and nuns, to found more usefully his college at Oxford with a school at Ipswich. He should have started earlier, and gone farther. The Cardinal's agent, Cromwell, took up the work and carried it out, perhaps too drastically.

From the demographic point of view there were far too many clerics, celibates, for the good of the country. The number needed considerable reducing. They were unproductive, living off the fat of the land they did little to increase – so much dead wood. The monasteries owned something like one-sixth of the land, far too top-heavy a structure for a subsistence economy to carry.

Ideally we might have preferred a couple of the best monasteries to have been retained in each county, for those who had such a vocation. This was not practical politics. To carry through so revolutionary a measure it was necessary to give head to the laity's hostility to the monasteries – one can observe that in every town from Canterbury to Bodmin – to appeal to the greed of the gentry to acquire Church lands, and to whip up Protestant animus against monasticism and clerical celibacy. It was originally intended to turn a dozen of the greater abbeys into cathedrals. But owing to the strain of Henry's third war with a France three or four times larger and richer than England, and with Scotland allied with France attacking on the Border, it was not possible to establish more than five or six as cathedrals. How much we miss such a splendid fane as Bury St Edmunds (another Ely), Glastonbury, Reading, Tavistock, Osney, or perhaps Abingdon, or Kirkstall!

Naturally the governing class was out for the lands of the Church. Froude points out that in the previous century there had been agitations for such a measure, and in Parliament too. For the most part it was a necessary measure to support the finances of the Crown, i.e. government. It is true that Henry was extravagant; but on the personal side much of the monastic resources went into building Renaissance palaces. The stones of Merton Abbey helped to build his fantasy palace of Nonesuch, a casualty of the Civil War. He added greatly to Wolsey's Whitehall and Hampton Court, and rebuilt St James's: the last two still enrich the dingy society of today.

Henry was a tremendous builder. We now know, from Howard Colvin's admirable researches, that Henry spent far more on the defence of the country: in his last years, 1539–1547, he spent £376,500 on fortifying the whole south coast with a defensive system of castles to protect harbours – more than he spent during the whole of his reign on his palaces. The castles and forts that guarded the Solent at Cowes and Calshot were built of stone from Beaulieu and Quarr abbeys. The lead from the houses of prayer went into guns, and Henry, personally interested in fortification and naval engineering, created the Navy.

The result was that, in the tough struggle of 1543–6, when Henry was left in the lurch by Charles V, the small country sustained the struggle with France alone and came through successfully, with the acquisition of Boulogne. The finances of the Crown, i.e. of government, were seriously strained; but the country, i.e. the governing class, prospered. The acquisition of church lands was a prime factor in the Rise of the Gentry to power, which enabled them to challenge the Crown itself in the next century. We should in fairness add that these lands, from being in the nerveless hands of a lot of reluctant celibates, gave rise to a notable increase in numbers and productive energy of the gentry. Hence the expansion at home and overseas, the energetic achievement of the Eliz-abethan Age.

Froude says little of all this, though it is implied in his wholly secular attitude towards the Reformation, and his enthusiasm for the exploits of the Elizabethan Seamen. A Sir Richard Grenville was based on Buckland Abbey, the church of which he transformed into a mansion; Drake bought it with the proceeds of his Voyage round the World. Henry's Lord Chancellor Wriothesley transformed Titchfield Abbey into a great house, posted there to keep an eye on Southampton – from which his title as Earl was derived. Another of Henry's ministers, Anthony Browne, converted Battle Abbey into a house; he also acquired the sites of Waverley and Bayham abbeys, and Eastbourne Priory: which enabled him to build his magnificent pile nearby at Cowdray, whence to keep an eye on the Sussex coast.

Now the interesting thing is that both the Wriothesley and Browne families remained Catholic – as Henry did, without the Pope. This should give pause to those who think in sectarian terms, instead of political. For myself, I think even more of the aesthe-tic losses of the Reformation, though there were gains on the secular side. Froude was not an aesthete, and says nothing of the shiploads of precious alabasters, vestments, textiles, parchments, books sent abroad; the sculpture, woodwork, carving, works of craftsmanship destroyed; the monastic libraries dispersed; the plate and bells melted down.

I blame Froude for this neglect; more, I disagree with his scale of values – putting action before art! But it would be too much to expect any thing else from a 19th century historian (except always Burckhardt), or perhaps even 20th century one.

Froude did not concern himself with economics, apart from prices and wages. He was opposed to the dominant economic orthodoxy of the age – *laissez-faire* and devil-take-the-hindmost. He had the historian's instinct that economic 'laws' are not eternal truths for all times and circumstances; in one essay he criticised Buckle for laying down such laws, pointing out that in history one can never precisely predict, and 'I object to all historical theories'. Events and people were all in all. Again and again in his work he inveighed against the free-market doctrines that prevailed. The 19th century, in England, gave no credit for intelligence to the 16th century view of economic policy, control of wages and prices, protection of the peasant against enclosure, the balance of trade against the drain of specie payments abroad – what became known later as Mercantilism.[1]

Here Froude had the support of Carlyle. Both cared more for the peasant than the capitalist (in my view mistakenly). Froude constantly praised country life as a better foundation for a society than the unhealthiness of urban life, especially of Victorian

---

1. Cunningham gave a more sympathetic and balanced view of Tudor economic policy in his *Growth of English Industry and Commerce*, I. c.1.

slums, and the demoralising conditions of conurbations.

We might take as a test case his treatment of the Pilgrimage of Grace, the one serious challenge to Henry's new deal and whole course of policy that these received. It came from the backward North, but diverse elements ran into it, economic and social grievances, political opposition, religious reaction, sympathy with the monasteries. Grievances were diverse in Lincolnshire, where the movement was started prematurely at Louth, from Yorkshire which became the heart of the resistance. Henry wrote of one of them angrily, 'Yea, and that the beastliest of the whole realm.' (We have had evidence of Yorkshire obstinacy in our own time). In Cumberland the agitation was chiefly against 'gressums', fines on entry upon leases, which were rising. To bring these varied elements together and unite them in a dangerous popular movement needed the ideological banner of religion. This was provided by the lawyer, Robert Aske, with whom it was undoubtedly sincere, and he proved to have a capacity for leadership. With Froude's inclination for men of action he treats him with marked respect, rebel as he was, and the narrative of the Rising is described vividly as Froude knew how.

'As he [Aske] rode down at midnight to the bank of the Humber, the clash of the alarm-bells came pealing far over the water. From hill to hill, from church tower to church tower, the warning lights were shooting. The fishermen on the German Ocean watched them flickering in the darkness from Spurnhead to Scarborough, from Scarborough to Berwick-upon-Tweed.

They streamed westward, over the long marshes across Spalding Moor; up the Ouse and the Wharfe to the watershed where the rivers flow into the Irish Sea. The mountains of Westmoreland sent on the message to Kendal, to Cockermouth, to Penrith, to Carlisle; and for days and nights there was one loud storm of bells and beacons from the Trent to the Cheviot Hills.'

Though this exemplifies Froude's fine sense of land-scape, I think we may see in it his response to Macaulay's famous ballad about the beacons lighting up the countryside at the approach of the Spanish Armada. Froude wrote some verse, but Macaulay wrote much better; indeed, he was that rarity – an historian who was also a good poet.

Froude treated the Pilgrimage essentially as a spon-taneous popular movement, in reaction to the new deal and the suppression of the monasteries, religious in character. Such it was in the mind of Robert Aske (his two brothers did not agree with him), and the monasteries had more respect in the North than they had, as the evidence shows, in the South. But politics entered into it, far more decisively than Froude could know at the time, in the persons of the conservative Opposition peers who pulled the strings from behind the scenes. Froude suspected Lord Darcy, who was responsible for order in the West Riding, as Lord Hussey, another collaborator, was for Lincolnshire. 'The extent of deliberate treachery on the part of Darcy may remain uncertain. The objects of the insurrection were cordially approved by him.' Thus much might have been guessed from the fact that the standard raised by the Pilgrims was Darcy's own private banner of the Five Wounds. He appeared to be dragging his feet when the rebellion broke in York-shire: in fact he was behind the whole thing.

Professor Elton has cleared up for us convincingly the political background of the Pilgrimage,[1] though we might have guessed much from the sophisticated political and religious demands put forward, quite beyond the aggrieved minds of a lot of peasants. At their back, instigating the movement, was a group of conservative politicals, strongest among the old peer-age, who hated Cromwell and the new deal. They hoped to bring pressure upon the King to get rid of him, re-instate the Lady Mary, and reverse the whole course approved by Parliament, by taking advantage of popular grievances in the discontented areas of the North. These were by no means all the North, but mainly Yorkshire, Cumberland, and part of Lincoln-shire. However, it was a critical time, the crisis of Henry's reign, for he knew well that the movement had the connivance of even more powerful members of the peerage, the Yorkist families of the Courtenays and the Poles, with their royal blood, and threatened support from abroad.

In our time the Pilgrimage of Grace has been treated almost wholly in sentimental terms, especially of course by Catholic historians, and rather absurdly by popular novelists. Once again, people hardly ever understand the politics behind historic events. In this crucial case Froude almost did; the State Papers had not yet been published, and not all the evidence was yet available. Yet he suspected Lord Darcy, when we

1.   G.R. Elton, 'Politics and the Pilgrimage of Grace', in B.C. Malament ed., *After the Reformation*, 26 foll.

now know the extent of his opposition: it was treason, and he rightly got his comeuppance. So too with the other leaders.

Froude was more sympathetic to the upright Robert Aske than is necessary: we do not have to sympathise with rebels upsetting society and order. It merely leads to unnecessary suffering and brings about the very things, more speedily and drastically, that they thought to prevent.

For what were the consequences of the Rebellion? Froude concludes simply: 'the insurgents were deceived by their strength. They believed themselves irresistible and, like many others who have played at revolutions, dreamt that they could afford to be moderate'. The poor fools! One consequence was that their action speeded up the suppression of the greater monasteries. Hitherto, by Act of Parliament, only the lesser houses with under £200 a year had been suppressed, and those of their inmates who wished to continue in religion drafted to the larger houses. Now the government's hand was strengthened to embark upon a campaign of getting all the greater monasteries to surrender, as if of their own volition; many were ready to do so, and now all monks and nuns were turned out into the world, though with pensions.

A further consequence was political. Froude deals with it in two chapters, 'The Commission of Cardinal Pole', and 'The Exeter Conspiracy'. Cardinal Pole, grandson of the Yorkist Clarence (murdered in the Tower on the orders of his brother, Edward IV), had been despatched by the Papacy to give leadership to the rebellion: his mission failed to coincide and he retired from the fiasco back upon Rome. But it brought his family and relatives into mortal danger. The French ambassador said that Henry intended to extinguish the whole house of the White Rose, and he very nearly succeeded. They were his most dangerous opponents: they had support from abroad, and they had a candidate for the throne, if anything untoward happened to the King, in the Lady Mary, who could be married to one of them.

Henry was well aware that he could not trust them. He could not trust his cousin, the Marquis of Exeter, like himself sprung from Edward IV, to go North and serve against the Pilgrims (he did not entirely trust the Duke of Norfolk, who had the command); so he sent Exeter West, really out of the way. He also dismissed the Marquis from intimate attendance upon him in his bedchamber, for the obvious reason: Exeter could have killed him. Instead of that, the Marquis was executed, along with the head of the Pole family, Lord Montague, on the evidence of another brother, Sir Geoffrey, who was pardoned, but escaped to Rome to receive absolution for his treachery to the family and his brother's death.

Such were the consequences of the Pilgrimage of Grace. Henry had surmounted the most dangerous internal crisis of his reign; but we see the reason for the strenuous programme of fortification and defence immediately embarked upon. This came just in time to confront the external crisis in the French war of 1543–6. Henceforward, Henry's most difficult task internally was to hold in leash the dynamic impulse of the Reformation which he had released. His problem was to keep the two parties in balance and maintain control; Froude himself speaks of the 'ungovernable

Reformers'. Henry was grievously worried by the bitter partisanship, which he could not stifle, and the breach of the national unity which he longed for.

He still had intense personal strains to undergo. There was the international humiliation of the Anne of Cleves fiasco, and the retribution that fell upon the author of it, his ablest minister. Then there was the miserable deception of his marriage to Catherine Howard, the candidate of the conservatives, with whom the ageing man was blissfully happy, until it fell to Cranmer to give him the evidence that he was being deceived. The old egoist was stunned, and could hardly bring himself to believe it; but there was no doubt about Catherine Howard's guilt, though every doubt about her cousin, Anne Boleyn's. Still the ageing man held on his course, continuing to lead his country; when he was too unwieldy and ill to move, he was carried in his wheel-chair down to Portsmouth to direct operations against the French fleet. He saw the *Mary Rose* overturn before his eyes, and, disregarding his own loss, gave himself to consoling the wife of the proud ship's commander. There was something irresistible, as well as resistible, about the man.

This it is that accounts for Archbishop Cranmer's always giving in, after some protest, to the King's needs and exigencies: he understood the inhuman strains upon the man, and in return Henry saved his life from his enemies. At Henry's death-bed Cranmer broke down in tears; the King could no longer speak, but he held his only friend's hand in his powerful grip until he died. Froude deeply disapproved of Macaulay's unworthy denigration of Cranmer. His own appreciation of the Archbishop may have owed something to his love of the language of Cranmer's Prayer Book (even Belloc appreciated that). Otherwise, it is somewhat unexpected, for Cranmer was not a man of action – the outspoken Latimer was more in his line.

Froude describes vividly, even touchingly, Henry's last appearance before Parliament and his speech grieving at the religious dissensions between one party and another. It was a plea for charity: 'this kind of man is depraved, and that kind of man; this ceremony and that ceremony. Of this I am sure, that charity was never so faint among you'. Henry was overcome with tears, perhaps partly of self-pity; for, years before, he had bewailed his lot at having to rule so unruly a nation. Many of the audience were in tears with him, as he descended from the throne for the last time, though little would be the effect, we can see from what happened when Henry was gone, upon the conduct of ordinary humans.

Henry had been a great leader, and the country was to feel the want of his strong hand upon the controls in the unstable and shifting sands of the middle of the century. Froude's summing-up seems fair enough. 'In his earlier life, though active and assiduous, he found leisure for elegant accomplishments.' Froude typically says nothing about Henry's love of music and singing, his composing songs and anthems, his taste in the arts – 'for splendid amusements, for relaxations careless, extravagant, sometimes questionable'. There speaks the Victorian moralist on a Renaissance prince. 'As his life drew onwards his lighter tastes disappeared, and the whole energy of his intellect was pressed into the business of the commonwealth.' Froude instanced the evidences of his work from printed sources, 'but only persons who have seen the original manuscripts, who have observed the traces of his pen in sidenotes and corrections, in drafts of Acts of Parliament, in expositions and formularies, in articles of faith, in Proclamations, in the countless multitudes of documents of all sorts, secular or ecclesiastical, which contain the real history of this extraordinary reign – only they can realise the extent of labour to which he sacrificed himself. His personal faults were great, and he shared besides them in the errors of his age; but . . . he sustained nobly the honour of the English name and carried the commonwealth securely through the hardest crisis in its history.'

The reception of this remarkable work was what might have been expected. In general it was unfavourable. The religious periodicals – and the Victorian age proliferated in them – responded according to their kind. Even apart from the prejudices of the third-rate, reviewers could not understand a work of genius: they thought that Froude's independence of mind was mere paradox. The *Edinburgh Review* embarked upon a bitter attack. Henry Reeve, the editor, was not a scholar and not qualified to judge; but he disliked Froude personally and 'shuddered at the glorification of a 'tyrant' like Henry VIII. He was a Whig of the most conventional type, regarding Macaulay and Hallam as the ideal historians, suspicious of novelty, and dismayed by paradox. *The Times* was an exception in the uproar, 'indeed was appreciative and sympathetic', and Froude was bucked by the understanding approval of another man of genius, Carlyle.

The response of the public was very different from that of ephemeral reviewers. 'The public took to

Froude's History from the first. The book sold as no history had sold, except Gibbon's and Macaulay's.' Naturally the inveterate Whig in Macaulay could not approve of the younger man's performance. But Froude had his own reservations about Macaulay; he acknowledged his brilliance, but deplored his 'indifference to truth and the recklessness of his statements', instancing his shocking injustice to the great Warren Hastings. (He might have added also to Clive, and to Marlborough – which angered Winston Churchill so much as to call Macaulay a 'liar'.)

Froude was a generation younger, eighteen years or so, than Macaulay, who died in 1859, leaving Froude in possession of the field.

Edwardians and Elizabethans

Froude's middle volumes on the reigns of Edward VI and Mary have usually been held the least controversial and disagreed with least. The reason is probably that the earlier volumes and the later are dominated respectively by the long reigns, and outsize personalities, of Henry VIII and Elizabeth I, and Froude's view of both gave rise to most disagreement. Henry had left the begetting of a son and heir too late, but hoped to maintain the balance he himself could command by appointing a Council from both sides, conservatives and progressives, to rule during the minority of his son, only nine when his father died. This attempt at control was immediately overthrown by the boy's uncle, Somerset, making himself Protector and assuming ascendancy. The dynamic impulse of Reform, with its attendant advantages to the Reformers, was to continue.

If anyone has any doubt about the necessity for a strong hand on the controls in time of revolution, he should have his eyes opened by the prodigious handout which the rapacious Council made to themselves during the six years of Edward's minority. Monastic lands, lands of the episcopal sees, and now the lands of the Chantries and ecclesiastical colleges – like the College at Stratford-on-Avon, Shakespeare's parish church – had been nationalised for the support of the Crown, i.e. to enable government to be carried on. Now a large proportion of these were annexed to themselves by the Councillors or purchased at low valuation, along with a grateful shower of grand titles to cover their nakedness with. As the Lady Mary, sulking in opposition, said on more than one occasion, 'My father made the more part of you out of almost nothing.' The Protector, the new Duke of Somerset, pulled down the cloisters of St Paul's, to build himself a palace in the Strand, Somerset House; at his West Country property of Berry Pomeroy we can still see, in ruins, the grand residence he raised within the old castle. So rebuilding went on all over the country, more usually making use of monastic buildings for the transformed residences.

For all this Froude gives figures, which naturally need revision after more than a century. He saw the significance of it all, and rightly drew the moral. 'The total value of the land which passed from the Crown in the reign of Edward VI, by gift, sale, or exchange, had been something over a million and a half.' He then goes into detail. 'After reasonable allowances for grants legitimately made as a reward for services, there will remain estates worth half-a-million [multiply for contemporary valuation], which the ministers of the Minority with their friends had appropriated – I suppose I must not say stolen – and divided among themselves. . . It appeared, in the inquiries which followed the deposition of Somerset from the Protectorate, that conveyances had been made out in other names to cover the extent of the appropriations. From the report as it stands Lord Paget and Sir

William Petre would seem to have made the smallest use of their opportunities, Lord Pembroke to have made the best.' The Protestant Pembroke settled himself handsomely upon the lands of Wilton nunnery; Paget and Petre made a no less handsome killing of monastic lands, and settled themselves richly, one at Beaudesert, the other at Ingatestone (with Thorndon too). These two were the ancestors of devout Catholic families, property being more important than opinions.

The historical significance of all this is that it provided the foundation for a new aristocracy alongside of the old. Froude understood this as well as any modern sociological historian. It is made quite clear, without any sociological jargon, in one of the best and most beautifully written of the Short Studies, 'Chenies and the House of Russell'. For that fortunate house was founded upon a large part of the possessions of Tavistock Abbey, along with Church properties in Exeter, Covent Garden and at Woburn.

On the side of religion Somerset was a sincere enough Protestant but Froude did not approve of his rash pushing forward of Reform. Somerset's personal high-handedness, along with the desire to be popular with the masses (he was not), appearing as a liberal probably genuinely enough, was not a recipe for good government. Good government is strong government. History is made by power and will power – no humbug about democracy from either Carlyle or Froude.

The reaction to Somerset's flaccid rule was what might be expected: two dangerous rebellions in one year, 1549, which cost a mint of money and the import of German mercenaries (always good at that) to put down. That in the West Country against the new Prayer Book was instigated by clerics with clerical demands. (When passing by the church of St Thomas's at Exeter, I always think of its Vicar, a tough customer and a fractious leader in the Rebellion, hanging from the top of his tower.) Ket's Rebellion in Norfolk was a social movement arising out of peasant grievances, enclosures, inflation, high prices, dearth. It was effectively put down by Warwick, who came forward as the alternative to Somerset, now falling from power, and who made himself Duke of Northumberland – with immense hand-outs in the North. The titles do not matter: it is the land that counts.

We must confine ourselves to Froude's treatment of these matters. He was sympathetic as ever to the grievances of the peasantry, and he was not unsympathetic to Somerset, to whom he gave credit for good intentions. Froude's account of agrarian problems is not essentially different from Tawney's, in *The Agrarian Problem in the Sixteenth Century*. 'A change in the relations between the peasantry and the owners of the soil, which three hundred years had but just effected – with the assistance of an unlimited field for emigration – was attempted harshly with no such assistance in a single generation.' Froude was all in favour of emigration to relieve population pressure in the 19th century: it was the right solution, as it still is today in a small overpopulated island, which has benefited from the results of emigration, been rescued by it, twice over in the German onslaughts of this century. Froude went on: 'the strictest canons of political economy do not give unrestricted scope to the rights of property. The

State claims an interest in the condition of the people which overrides personal privileges.'

Nor had he any illusions about the dynamic of the Reformation impulse, opted for by Northumberland as a matter of politics, when such little religious belief as he had was Catholic. Froude describes what happened, vividly as ever, with the added rhetoric of disgust. 'Northumberland, following the steps of his father who filled the treasury of Henry VII and brought his own head to the block, set himself to the work with heart and goodwill. In the autumn and winter of 1552–3 no less than nine commissions were appointed with this one object; four of which were to go again over the often-trodden ground and glean the last spoils which could be gathered from the churches. In the business of plunder the rapacity of the Crown officials had been distanced hitherto by private peculation. The halls of country-houses were hung with altar cloths; tables and beds were quilted with copes.' At Hardwick Hall today one sees the Elizabethan textiles made out of the almuces of copes, and Froude was right that chalices were made into secular goblets. 'There was one special commission for bells, vestments, and ornaments; two for plate and jewels; a fourth to search private houses for church property.' In addition to the losses of sculpture and woodwork, the destruction of shrines and images which had begun under Henry VIII, the churches were now denuded and swept bare. It is true that secular persons, nobility and gentry, profited immensely, but much too went abroad.

It may surprise people who think of Froude as simply pro-Protestant – in effect he was, but not 'simply' –

that he approved of Charles V's Interim, taking a moderate, tolerant position, something between doctrinaire Protestantism and the fanatical Counter-Reformation. 'In a worldly sense the Protestants would have been more prudent had they taken the Emperor at his word. The Interim was in theory as liberal as the scheme of belief as yet established in England. In practice it was even more liberal, for the marriage of the clergy, though censured, was not forbidden. . . A considerable liberty of opinion might have established itself under the shelter of the Interim. But the Germans, more spiritual than the English [so they have always thought themselves] were less tolerant of compromise.'

It is this that accounts, again surprisingly, for Froude's high opinion of Paget, as the ablest brain on the Council, when Paget was really a *politique*, a latitudinarian in religion – the cleverest mind (except for Cecil), also the humblest born among these mostly new men. Here we must cite Froude on judgment in history. 'In contemplating the false steps of statesmen, it is difficult at all times to measure their personal responsibility, to determine how much of their errors has been due to party spirit, how much to pardonable mistake. How much again seems to have been faulty because we see but effects, which we ascribe absolutely to the conduct of particular men, when such effects were the result, in fact, of influences spreading throughout the whole circle of society.'

This is rare historical wisdom. Just as Macaulay owed much as an historian to his experience of government in India and in England, what G.M. Trevelyan called his 'tall measure of events', so Froude was no armchair academic. A member of the governing class, a friend of statesmen such as Derby and Caernarvon, Froude understood the problems of government, immensely more adult and sophisticated than easy radical protest. (Any fool can criticise, but can he do the job?) We should add here another consideration: there are some situations in history that cannot be got right, or put right, even when the problem is clear enough and the right solution indicated. We have only to look round the world today to see situations of the sort on every hand, and all through Froude's life he was brought close to such a case in the history of Ireland.

Northumberland was caught in such a situation with the young Edward VI dying on his hands. Nobody had expected that – what was he to do, what course take? Froude was hard on Northumberland. Like Henry VIII, he was a *faux-bonhomme*; and he was able. A French ambassador said that there were only two men capable of governing the country for Edward: Somerset and Northumberland. The former had failed.

Once more we must cite Froude on the importance of the individual in history against the background of mass-considerations, so much to the fore at the time in the work of Buckle. (Lenin said that 'Politics begin with the masses'; but the Russian Revolution would not have taken the form it did but for him as an individual.) 'Philosophers, who believe that great events are enveloped in great causes, that the future is evolved out of the present by laws unerring as those which regulate the processes of nature, can see in the grandest of individual men but instruments which might easily have been dispensed with. Centuries, it may be, take their complexion from these large influences, and broad laws of progress may shape the moulds for the casting of eras; but the living English-man of the 16th century would have seen in these closet speculations but the shadow of a dream com-pared with the interests which depended on the result of the illness of a boy who was not yet sixteen. The eyes of England, of the Emperor, of the Pope, of the King of France, of all the civilised world, were turned to the sick-bed at Greenwich.'

We all know what happened. Contrary to expect-ations the sickly Lady Mary came to the throne, and attempted to put back the clock to where it had been twenty years before. The attempt was an impossible one; clever Edwardians, like the Lady Elizabeth, William Cecil and others waited until the hiatus was over. Neither Mary nor Cardinal Pole had good actuarial prospects, and her ablest minister, Bishop Gardiner (who had been up to his eyes in the divorce proceedings against her mother) died half-way through the hiatus. The Reformation dynamic could not have been held up any more than a geological fault can.

We must not repeat the familiar story: there is a new historical point to be made here. Northumberland has always been blamed for forcing the young Edward VI to wrest the succession away from his half-sister Mary. From the recent work of Professor W.K. Jordan on the reign, it does not appear that Edward needed to be forced. Well-educated, cool-headed, intelligent, he already showed a strong Tudor will of his own, and he was a convinced, priggish Protestant, who deeply resented his Catholic sister's resistance to the laws of the realm. His Protestant half-sister, Elizabeth, conformed as she was to conform to the (different) laws under Mary. But both princesses had been declared bastards, and they could hardly both be legitimate. Edward preferred his indubitably legitimate, and indubitably Protestant, cousin, Lady Jane Grey – also highly educated and intelligent. She would have made a good queen, better than poor Mary. The dying Edward himself forced the Council to sign up his Device for the Succession, Archbishop Cranmer reluctantly, while clever Cecil said that he signed only as a witness. The country preferred the daughters of Henry VIII, and to follow his Will – in its way a tribute to the old monster.

It is an interesting thought that, but for the death of the young King, we should have had an Edwardian age instead of an Elizabethan. All the leading Elizabethans were really Edwardians, formed and coloured by the experience of those critical years, rendered more cautious by it: Elizabeth herself and Cecil, Nicholas Bacon and Archbishop Parker (who had preached to Ket's rebels at Mousehold Heath), young Lord Robert Dudley to become the princely Leicester, Henry Sidney, viceroy in Elizabethan Wales and Ireland, in whose arms Edward had died.

Mary's brief reign was decisive, in this sense: it proved that England could not be governed on that basis, full Papal Catholicism, any longer. It was a failure at home and abroad; by the time Mary and Pole died London was practically ungovernable. Mary could produce no heir, and – bitterest irony – had to close the ports against a Papal condemnation of the Cardinal – for all that he had done to revive subjection to Rome. The burnings of some 288 poor souls did not quench the increase of Protestantism, but the fatal Spanish marriage – with its subordination of English interests to Philip's and the unforgivable and unforgiven loss of Calais – stoked the fires of patriotism. The intense opposition to Philip's arrival – perhaps this was why he landed at Southampton instead of Plymouth – produced insurrection in the West Country, especially among Protestant sea-going families, Carews, Killigrews, Champernownes, Tremaynes. We find those families favoured and making their mark under Elizabeth. From this time free-booting in the Channel got free scope; Plymouth developed close links with Huguenot La Rochelle;[1] the Elizabethan Seamen were on the way across the Atlantic.

All this was grist to Froude's mill. Born and bred on the Dart, neighbour and friends with the Champernownes, Gilberts, Carews and Tremaynes, Froude paid tribute to them in his History and devoted other writings to their exploits. They appealed to his patriotism, and the gravamen of his charge against the rule of Mary and Pole was that it was anti-patriotic: it subordinated England's interests to Spain. In internal affairs Mary, a passionate Spanish *dévote*, favoured the Church, devoting what resources of the Crown she could to reparation – the restoration of monks at Westminster Abbey, of friars elsewhere – and Froude considered that more important interests, the nation's, suffered.

Again we must distinguish between the personal

---

1. cf. J.A. Williamson's excellent biography of Sir John Hawkins.

and the political. No doubt the majority of people were still Catholics. What does that matter? It is the balance of power in the governing class that counts – in London, the South and East, the gentry and bourgeois nuclei in the towns, the universities – not in the backwoods. Froude had no personal animus against Mary, (as he certainly had against Mary Queen of Scots); he felt pity for the sadness of her frustrated life, the sorrows she had experienced over years. He gave more respect than necessary to people deluded by their beliefs, when it is their beliefs that make fools of men, and women. What he disliked in Pole was his Counter-Reformation dogmatism – the earlier Pole had been more of a humanist, and, before the Revolution, something of a reformer, like More. I do not think Froude knew fully what a persecutor St Thomas More became, certainly not the full tale of his vendetta against Lutherans.

Froude contrasted Pole's Italianate oratory unfavourably with the simple homespun English of the Marian Martyrs, recorded by Foxe. In a footnote he pinpointed Pole's casuistry in an exchange of letters with Cranmer – and we should dutifully note the increase of footnotes as the great History proceeded on its way, largely from the foreign archives in the study of which Froude led the way. Are we right in seeing his reaction to Newman's subtle casuistry in one footnote, or to his experience of the Oxford Movement in his characterisation of the Cardinal? 'His character was irreproachable; in all the virtues of the Catholic Church he walked without spot or stain; and the system to which he had surrendered himself had left to him of the common selfishnesses of mankind his enormous vanity alone. [Manning said of Newman that his trouble was 'pride'.] That system had exting- uished also in him the human instincts, the genial emotions by which theological theories stand especial- ly in need to be corrected. He belonged to a class . . . of men of an 'idea'; who unable to accept things as they are, are passionate loyalists, passionate church- men, passionate revolutionists' – in one word, idea- logues.

I quote this passage to illustrate the point of view from which Froude wrote his History. He makes an original point in regard to the burning of Cranmer, which Macaulay had not thought of. After a vivid description of the appalling scene in the ditch outside the city wall at Oxford – not far from the Martyrs' Memorial erected to spite the Oxford Movement – Froude reflects: 'he was brought out, with the eyes of his soul blinded [poor Cranmer had wavered to and fro in his beliefs, between various nonsense-propositions] to make sport for his enemies, and in his death he brought upon them a wider destruction than he had effected by his teaching while alive. . . The Court had over-reached themselves by their cruelty. Had they been contented to accept the recantation, they would have left the Archbishop to die broken-hearted, pointed at by the finger of pitying scorn. And the Reformation would have been disgraced in its cham- pion.' Then Froude adds his own personal conviction: 'The worth of a man must be measured by his life, not by his failure under a single and peculiar trial.'

For a gloss upon Froude's viewpoint we may take his comment upon Cecil's going to mass, and taking a confessor into his household, under Queen Mary.

Clever people like him and the Lady Elizabeth conformed to the law of the land and went to mass, not to the stake. Cecil had been a secretary of state under Edward VI, but took 'no formal part in Mary's government'. She was, in fact, hard put to it to find able servants in either her church or state. 'In religion Cecil, like Paget, was a latitudinarian', says Froude. This is incorrect. Paget *was* a latitudinarian, who ultimately settled for Catholicism. Cecil was a good Protestant, who did not think it worth being burnt for it, sensible man. Martyrs like More are only too ready to martyrise others. As Froude says, 'as long as that creed [the Catholic] was the law of the land, as a citizen Cecil paid the law the respect of external obedience. . . It was the view of common sense. It was not the view of a saint.'

William Cecil was not a saint, but an upright man of sound judgment and immense ability. He would not serve Queen Mary's government in anything but a subordinate capacity; for her part she paid him the tribute, 'Cecil is an honest man.' Thus he waited – to become the architect of the success of Elizabeth I's reign.

Froude had intended at first to write the history of Elizabeth I's long reign, but in the end, after half-a-dozen volumes decided to finish at the Spanish Armada in 1588.[1] I think he got tired of her and her ways, her tergiversations and difficulty in making up her mind, her feminine deviousness and arts, her poses and tantrums, her exhibitionism for ever playing to

1. The original edition was in twelve volumes; my references are to the Everyman edition in ten.

the gallery, her indirectness and what he considered her insincerity. The result was that, paradoxically, the champion of the Reformation in England did grave injustice to the woman who saw it through to success. She was not simple enough for him. In my view this is the chief blot upon his work. Froude's junior in the field, Bishop Creighton, had a better understanding of the woman and did her justice in his biography of her. Though he had not Froude's genius, he was a cleverer man, and, an ecclesiastical statesman, he was trained in the arts of the Renaissance Papacy and the crafts of Italian Popes. (Elizabeth had a dash of Visconti blood through her Valois descent, and, a remarkable linguist among other things, was proud of her Italian.)

Froude began well enough on her. 'There was a capacity in her for great self-sacrifice. [She sacrificed her sex-life as a woman to her duty as a sovereign.] Conscious of her power over herself, she liked to dally with temptation; but she remained at all times mistress of her passions. And to steer the English nation in the midst of the breakers was a keener enjoyment to her than to listen to the soft dalliance of a Robert Dudley.' This was no more than just, and the image true to Froude. Then, 'a Protestant, in the sense that Cecil was a Protestant, Elizabeth never to the last became.' This was also true. Hers was an undoctrinal religion, akin to that of the greatest writer of her age, who thought that one cannot box up the incomprehensible mystery of life and the universe in a set of dogmas: 'We are such stuff As dreams are made on, and our little life Is rounded with a sleep.' Accepting, as he did, a moral order of the universe, she was genuinely open-minded, as he was.

The manly man preferred the manly John Knox, incomprehensibly to us; and Knox had no high opinion of Elizabeth either, 'neither good Papist nor sound Protestant.' She knew how to deal with that trouble-maker: she kept him out of her country. Mary Stuart could not – she should not have mis-conducted herself and allowed him to win: Elizabeth would never have done. Mary did well enough in Scotland, until sex raised its ugly head in the potent shape of Bothwell. Mary Stuart, of the able Guise family, was essentially French and never was *au fait* with English feeling; Elizabeth was a great-great-granddaughter, through her mother, of a Lord Mayor of London and had her feet firmly on bourgeois ground. As Cecil knew, and Creighton well understood, Elizabeth's heart-beat instinct for the English people was one of her prime qualifications for ruling them.

A large part of the second volume on the reign is devoted to Scottish affairs, exceptionally for a History of England. Throughout there are visual flashes equal to Macaulay's. 'The dying Mary of Lorraine [Mary Stuart's mother, ruling for her daughter married in France] had been carried from her bed to the walls of the Castle to watch the fight. As the sun rose out of the Forth, she saw the English columns surge like the sea-waves against the granite ramparts, and like the sea-waves fall shattered into spray.' Froude's tell-tale sea-image again.

The French of the Auld Alliance – were extruded for good from Scotland, and for the first time for centuries England enjoyed security at her back-door on the Borders. This was Cecil's prime achievement. He had had to threaten resignation to force Elizabeth

to intervene; cautious, after her experiences under
Edward VI and her narrow escape from death in the
Tower under her sister, Elizabeth had hesitated to the
last. The second occasion when he, backed by the
whole Council and Parliament, forced her hand was
over the execution of Mary Stuart. Driven to the end
of her resources by 'the daughter of debate' – as she
called Mary, who had conspired against her life and
throne, Elizabeth had a virtual breakdown, and the
Council practically took the decision out of her hands.

Cecil was handsomely rewarded for his victory in
Scotland. The Queen was not ungenerous, but, careful of the nation's resources, kept her eye on expend-
iture to the end of her days – like her grandfather,
unlike her extravagant father. Besides she well knew
how much the new men had purloined from the
resources of Crown and nation during her brother's
minority: how many families to become famous in
history were based upon it: Seymours, Sidneys, Her-
berts, Russells, Cavendishes, Wriothesleys, Monta-
gues, Cecils. William Cecil made an immense fortune,
legitimately for his life-long service, but enough to
found two branches of the family, the senior at palatial
Burghley, the junior at no less palatial Theobalds
exchanged by his younger son for Hatfield. Froude
does not make much of this; neither have subsequent
historians, except Catholic partisans like Belloc and
Chesterton.

Froude's third volume has the crisis of the reign to
deal with: the complicated events of the three years
1569–72, interlocked opposition at home and danger
from abroad: the Duke of Norfolk, Elizabeth's own
cousin's involvement in the Ridolphi Plot against her;

then his conspiring to marry Mary with an eye on Elizabeth's throne; the Queen excommunicated by the Pope and 'deposed', her Catholic subjects absolved from their allegiance to her; the Rising of the Northern Earls, Northumberland and Westmorland. Since Elizabeth would do nothing about the succession, one-half of her Council went over to the idea of a Mary Stuart–Norfolk marriage as a solution. Elizabeth knew too well from experience what that would mean: she said that within a month she would see the inside of the Tower again.

Throughout the prolonged crisis the Queen and Cecil held together against a majority of the Council and the nobility, Catholic and Protestant. But they had the sense of the country with them, their fingers on the pulse of the nation, and eventually the backing of Parliament, which wanted to bring Mary to the block. Elizabeth would not stand for that; after long hesitation she compromised, allowing the traitor Norfolk's condemnation to be carried out.

This was the watershed of the reign; after it there was no further doubt that the new deal would be carried forward. An interesting sign, the mass-vestments which had been put away in many places, at All Souls, for instance – in hope of another day, an about-turn – were brought out and sold. Archbishop Parker, who had been Anne Boleyn's chaplain, made the College sell them and invest the proceeds in land: a good thing.

All this makes for an exciting volume, though Froude spares half a chapter on 'The Economic Condition of the Country'. The misery of the middle decades of the century was passing; the stability and

61

lenity of Elizabeth's government, along with Gresham's stabilisation of the currency, led to a marked increase of trade. The lands of the Church, in the more energetic hands of the gentry, providing for younger sons and establishing more such families, were rendered more productive. 'While the political and religious passions of the English nobility were increasing in heat and intensity', says Froude, 'the economical condition of the commons was slowly improving. The social convulsions which accompanied the earlier stages of the Reformation had settled down. The State Papers are no longer crowded with complaints of the oppression of the poor.' Today we have more precise evidence that the value of land was going up as it became more productive, and Cecil watched over every aspect of the country's increasing wealth and resources with paternal care.

In the very next paragraph Froude makes this point: 'It was fortunate for Elizabeth that another occupation was open to them [the energetic sons of these families] – that the sea-going portion of her subjects were those in whom the ideas of the Reformation had taken the deepest root; and that the merchant therefore could change his character for that of the buccaneer with the approval of his conscience as well as to the advantage of his purse.' Evidently Froude saw the connection, though he does not spell it out in the economic terms of modern sociological historiography.

He was now more than half-way through his immense task and a more experienced writer. At the outset of this volume he gives us a clear statement of the principle that guided his writing. 'The philosophy of history which resolves events into the action of organic and necessary laws, conceals from us the perplexities of the living instruments by which those events were brought about. We see what actually happened; we imagine that we discern the causes which determined the effects. And, in assuming a necessary connection between them, we smile at the needless fears, we ridicule the needless precautions of kings and ministers. We despise them as short-sighted; we censure them as arbitrary and tyrannical. . . . By a subtle process of intellectual injustice, we convert the after-experience of facts into principles of reasoning which would have enabled us to foresee those facts; and we infer, with unconscious complacency, the superiority of modern intelligence.'

'Knowledge of the result', a wise man once observed, 'has spoilt the composition of history.' A just moral appreciation of conduct is made impossible by it. 'The remedy, so far as there is a remedy, is to look wherever we can through the eyes of contemporaries from whom the future was concealed.'

This is a salutary warning to us arm-chair historians from one who knew how history happens. The greatest of arm-chair historians, S.R. Gardiner, took it to heart and made it the governing principle of his blameless History of England in the 17th century. He exemplifies the principle better than Froude himself did. On the other hand Froude buttressed himself by long quotations from contemporary documents and footnotes citing the originals – though again he was criticised, as he was criticised for everything he wrote.

In Volume IV Froude pays a tribute to Elizabeth's financial policy – clue to the success of her reign; Philip II, with all the treasures of the Indies at command, twice went bankrupt, overstraining his resources to intervene everywhere. 'Elizabeth was sparing, on principle, of her subjects' purses as well as her own; after all, when the demands upon the treasury from France, from Flanders, from Scotland, the expenses of the Navy and of the fortifications on the coast, are considered against the revenue, the wonder is rather at the greatness of the results which Elizabeth achieved. . . . However it was, she did succeed with combined courage and cunning in holding at bay the Catholic powers. England, with peace and immunity from taxation, grew enormously in wealth and strength, and the Queen herself was gaining a hold on the affections of her subjects' – if not on Froude's.

He proceeds to pay a reluctant tribute to her on the score of religion. 'Events were too strong for her. Her theory was two centuries before its time, and nations can only be governed on principles with which they sympathise themselves.' This should not mean that the tolerationism of this highly intelligent and civilised woman was wrong, and the mutual exclusiveness of uncivilised fanatics right! 'Yet Elizabeth may be fairly credited with a general rectitude of purpose; and for the immediate purpose of keeping England quiet and preventing civil war, she was acting prudently and successfully.' This is no more than just. Everybody in Europe, even her enemies, recognised that the English government was the most efficient and successful of the time.

'On the same principle on which she prohibited Puritan conventicles and forbade Catholics to preach in public or say mass, she checked the tongues of the

Reformers in Parliament.' Modern historians, with their Parliamentarian perspective and Leftist tradition, are all too friendly towards Puritan troublemakers; apart from anything else, they are being anachronistic, not seeing the trouble caused in the dangerous circumstances of the time. Even eminent historians like G.M. Trevelyan and Samuel Eliot Morison, let alone lesser ones, have been far too simply pro-Puritan. Froude says, 'while secular questions were best resolved by debate [in Parliament], religious animosities she always attempted to suffocate.' Was she not right? Give ordinary people freedom to air their mutually contradictory opinions – as 'Truth', and the next thing they would be at each other's throats. The devastation wrought by the religious wars in France and the Netherlands brought this home at the time; after a blissful interval England herself was to go through a similar experience with the Puritan Revolution and the Civil War.[1]

Having allowed thus much, Froude now went wrong about her and the Elizabethan Church, in pages where I must flatly contradict him. 'She always advised the Netherlands to make no alterations in religion.' That was wise, and would have saved the Netherlands decades of agony and oceans of bloodshed. Then, 'having no belief herself, she regarded Protestantism as a lost cause.' This is plain wrong: she was not an unbeliever but an undoctrinal Anglican, an Erasmian – and how much better off Europe would have been if it had followed Erasmus, instead of Luther and Calvin!

---

1. For the appalling consequences cf. my *Reflections on the Puritan Revolution*.

There follows an unjustified attack on the Elizabethan Church, particularly the episcopate. 'Her bishops she treated with studied insolence as creatures of her own, whom she had made and could unmake at pleasure: the bishops themselves lived as if they knew their day to be a short one, and made the most of their opportunities while they lasted. Scandalous dilapidations, destruction of woods, waste of the property of the sees by beneficial leases, each incumbent enriching himself and his family at the expense of his successors – this is the substantial history of the Anglican hierarchy, with a few honourable exceptions, for the first twenty years of its existence.'

Well, it is not. A tradition of flinging mud at the Elizabethan episcopate has come down to us, and it is quite unjustified. I know most of the Elizabethan bishops, and there was only one bad lot among them – Marmaduke Middleton, a Welsh gent. He was very properly degraded by the Court of High Commission (which Puritans disapproved and attacked). The bulk of the Elizabethan bishops were overworked beasts of burden, upon whom the State unloaded all kinds of secular chores in addition to having to administer their dioceses, and keep up hospitality in their mostly impoverished sees. I know of only one episcopal family that edged itself into the peerage – that of Sandys; and, though the Queen disliked clerical marriage, this family justified itself in its remarkable progeny. For all his Puritan bias, Christopher Hill gives a more just account in his *Economic Condition of the Church*.

The fact is that, as time went on, Froude became more unsympathetic, positively unjust, to both Queen and Church.[1] In later studies he seems to express a positive distaste for the Church of England. He regarded it as a mish-mash, neither one thing nor the other. This was to miss the whole point of it – which was, on the negative side, to bridge the gap between Catholic and Protestant, blur the sharp edges in its comprehension, and, from a positive angle, to bring out what was better on each side. As such, it has historically carried, and expressed, the character of the English people, as neither Rome nor Geneva could do.

In this volume, covering the 1570's and 1580's, Ireland comes to the fore, and Froude devotes two long chapters to Irish affairs. 'To preserve some kind of clearness in a narrative where the threads are so many and so confused, I have set apart the history of Ireland for separate treatment' – and we will follow suit. 'Although', he says, 'the condition of that country affected materially the action of Elizabeth's government, and prevented the Queen from assuming the bolder position which circumstances so many times appeared to thrust upon her. What the Low Countries were to Spain Ireland was to England: a dependent province occupied by a population alien in blood, creed, and in temperament. The vulnerable point where foreign princes were sure of welcome who offered to assist the people in shaking off their oppressors.'

The strategic consideration was decisive; Spain could have afforded to disengage herself from the Netherlands with far greater safety to herself than ever England could afford to disengage herself from Ireland.

---

1. And cf. the concluding reflection in the History, V. 472.

With the sharpening of the international conflict and the outbreak of war with Spain, Froude's last volume deals mainly with foreign affairs. The Protestant leaders had been assassinated in France and Scotland; there were continual plots against Elizabeth's life. With the assassination of the Dutch leader, William the Silent, and the dispatch of Parma with an efficient Spanish army to extinguish Dutch resistance, England was forced to intervene in the Netherlands, for strategic reasons above all. Throughout her modern history England has never been able to accept the threat of a great power entrenched across the vital sea-approaches to London. Reluctantly Elizabeth accepted the dour necessity, and for the rest of her life was burdened by the struggle.

Froude puts it ungenerously thus. 'She refused the place which belonged to her at the head of a Protestant confederation.' But that was not her duty, which was to look after the interests of her own country. I think we may see a Victorian inflexion in Froude's misconception of the situation – at its worst in his friend, the simple-minded Motley's popular *The Rise of the Dutch Republic*. This purist New Englander gives a very hostile account of England's prolonged efforts to save Dutch independence – successful only after decades of struggle implying they might have done better for themselves. The Dutch state, with its brilliant record in modern history, would never have come into existence, or survived, if it had not been for England's intervention and help, militarily, navally, and financially.

This was the fundamental reason for the war with Spain, and of course England was looking after her

own interests too – what did the innocent, pro-
Prussian Motley, the friend of Bismarck, expect?
Elizabeth's political sense determined her not to be
dragged at the tail of the Dutch, putting the limited
resources of her country into the bottomless sea of
their demands. As against simple Motley the clever
Canning summed up later:

> The fault of the Dutch
> Is in giving too little
> And asking too much.

Elizabeth wisely kept the conditions of her intervention, and the magnitude of her support, under her own
control. And this against the demands of Leicester, in
command of the English army there, supported by
practically the whole of the Council at home.[1] This
critical affair in itself shows up her decisive rôle in
government, when it came to the crunch. Cecil knew
better than Froude and historians who mistake the
matter: Cecil at the end of his life instructed his clever
son Robert, who took over, never to press the Queen
beyond her own judgment, her knowledge and experience were such.

Thus we come, at the end of his great work, to his
famous, and unfair, summing-up. 'Vain as she was of
her own sagacity, she never modified a course recom-
mended to her by Burghley [William Cecil] without
injury to the realm and to herself. She never chose an

---

1. For the crisis in more detail, v. my *The England of Elizabeth*,
   273–5; and c. x, 'Intervention in the Netherlands', in *The
   Expansion of Elizabethan England*.

opposite course without plunging into embarrass-
ments, from which his skill and Walsingham's were
able to extricate her.' All that is true here is, what
Burghley and Walsingham complained sometimes,
that when things went ill they got the blame, when
they went well she took the credit. That was very
natural, and right for a sovereign – part of the game.

Froude concluded that 'the great results of her reign
were the fruits of a policy which was not her own, and
which she starved and mutilated when energy and
completeness were most needed.' This is not the less
wrong for having been often quoted. The manly man
in Froude was all for action; Elizabeth as a woman
could always say No – as Henry VIII never could, who
fancied himself as a military commander (More saw
that clearly), and thus strained the country's resources, which his daughter always sought to preserve
and strove to nourish.

Perhaps Froude was tired after twenty years of hard
labour, while at the same time editing *Fraser's* and
writing a great deal – many of his *Short Studies* – for it.
He was ready to end with the Armada, which was at
any rate one of the decisive events of history, for it
announced the arrival of a first-rate sea-power which
could stand up to the resources of imperial Spain. It
opened the way to the future. This is the implication
of Froude's curious last words, ending on no high
dramatic note. As against what Dean Inge regarded as
Newman's 'horrible' concept of education as 'to pour
Truth into a child's mind and then seal it up in
perpetuity', Froude opted for flexibility and progress:
'the worst legacy which princes or statesmen could
bequeath to their country would be the resolution of

all its perplexities, the establishment once and for ever of a finished system, which would neither require nor tolerate improvement.' That way lay the decadence of Spain, after its *siglo d'oro*.

In the course of so long a work Froude gave expression to his general reflections on history, and we have seen that, as with all works that have life in them, he was in part reacting against the topical developments, the issues and preferences, perhaps the ideology, of his own time. What he has to say about the Victorian unleashing of democracy and the rôle of violence in history is still topical. 'Always and everywhere, even among the bravest peoples, the majority are spiritual cowards; and had England in the 16th century been governed by universal suffrage, the Roman Catholic system, considered as a rule of opinion, could not have been overthrown without violence. . . Government by suffrage however is possible only in periods when the convictions of men have ceased to be vital to them. [Perhaps not even then – look around the world today!] As long as there is a minority which would rather die . . . when ten men are so earnest on one side that they will sooner be killed than give way, and twenty are earnest enough on the other to cast their votes for it but will not risk their skins, the ten will give the law to the twenty. . . .'

The Victorians did not much care for this straight talk, and liberals were infuriated by this historian's questioning their pet assumptions. Froude knew more history than they did, indeed his was a point of view which was framed and dominated by history: he knew that force and will and power were more important than votes in the making of history. And in his own time there were Fenian bombs and assassinations to remind people of the facts about human nature, as does the IRA today.

In his letters we can peep behind the scenes, see what he thought about his task, and how he set about it. Conscientiously he visited the scenes which he was to write about, and thus so vividly. To Skelton in Scotland: 'You must take me to Lochleven [whence Mary Queen of Scots escaped from confinement]. I want to make out Carberry Hill, and to seat myself on Queen Mary's stone. . . . And then to Stirling, Perth, and Glasgow. Before I go farther I must have a personal knowledge of Lochleven Castle and the grounds at Langside. Also I must look at the street at Linlithgow where Moray was shot.' We should allow that travelling then – especially in Scotland – was not so easy as now. 'The story grows wilder and grander the more I know of it; but like most wild countries it has bad roads through it, and the travelling is dangerous. . . . Afterwards I must go to Carlisle, and see Naworth and the Border-line to Berwick.'

It is not easy to conceive today, how much of the story Froude had to tell was imperfectly known, and how much was new that he brought out from years of work, all told, in archives at home and abroad. To Lady Salisbury: 'I am slowly drawing to the end of my long journey through the Records. By far the largest part of Burghley's papers is here, and not at Hatfield.' Correct: Burghley's papers are mainly in the Lansdowne Ms. in the British Library. It is Robert Cecil's papers that formed most of the great mass of papers at Hatfield, subsequently published by the Historical

Manuscripts Commission. Froude worked mainly from the manuscripts themselves. Then, 'I have been incessantly busy in the Record Office. . . . I am now sufficiently master of the story to be able to make very good (I dare say complete) use of the Hatfield papers. I feel as if there were very few dark places left in Queen Elizabeth's proceedings anywhere. I substantially end, in a blaze of fireworks, with the Armada. The concentrated interest of the reign lies in the period now under my hands. It is all action, and I shall use my materials badly if I cannot make it as interesting as a novel.' That had been Macaulay's aim too, and Froude may have been consciously recalling his words.

He got special permission to work in the Spanish archives at Simancas, where few can have penetrated before the discouragingly difficult handwritings in several languages; still Froude was not discouraged. He had very little help, except during one stay there from a brother-in-law. 'Often at the end of a page I have felt as after descending a precipice. I had to cut my way through a jungle, for no-one had opened the road for me. I have been turned into rooms piled to the window-sill with bundles of dust-covered despatches, and told to make the best of it. Often I have found the sand glistening on the ink where it had been sprinkled when a page was turned. There the letter had lain, never looked at again since it was read and put away.'

Hence something of the excitement which entered into his narrative. I have, very rarely, had a similar experience myself with old documents; but in our day roads have been cut through the jungle for us, in the immense piles of printed publications – and much of the excitement lost.

Ireland

Everything about Ireland is controverted, though not everything about the subject is controversial. One thing that cannot be gainsaid is that, throughout the modern period (until our nuclear era), England could not disengage herself from Ireland, if only for strategic reasons. Ireland was her Achilles' heel. In all the wars of the 16th, 17th and 18th centuries, her Continental enemies time and again tried to make use of Ireland to get at England: Spain under Philip II and Philip III, France under Louis XIV and the French Revolution.

Internally, there are two ways of regarding Irish history: the Celtic, and the Anglo-Saxon. A Celt myself, I am not qualified to take the Celtic point of view, since I do not know the language, neither did Froude; few people did in the 19th century. Anyway, he was a Teutonist with an exaggerated view of the virtues of the Germanic races, like all 19th century historians. And the worst of them was his mentor, Carlyle (though, paradoxically, with a name like that, he must have been a Celt). Unlike Matthew Arnold, more than half a Celt himself,[1] Froude had not much Celtic sympathy and no high opinion of Celtic charac-

1.   v. my *Matthew Arnold, Poet and Prophet.*

ter or temperament, though he was not the worst offender.

We can rise above these prejudices, by taking a more objective, if not impartial, point of view, like that of Archbishop David Mathew's *Celtic Peoples and Renaissance Europe*. In that perceptive book he saw the process of the new Renaissance state emerging out of the mess of the Middle Ages, inevitably with its energy encroaching upon the backward, often pre-medieval, Celtic societies around the western rim of Europe. France was encroaching upon Brittany, even the puny Scottish state infiltrating into the Highlands; England, with energy reinforced by the Reformation, was ineluctably pushing forward in Ireland, with Henry VIII and Elizabeth I, a propulsion comparable to, and even linked with, that across the Atlantic to the coasts of America.

We must not become bogged down in the variegated morass of Irish history, but confine ourselves to what Froude made of it. In the first place, he was well acquainted with the country and people, and loved Irish landscape – with temperamental exaggeration, he thought it the most beautiful in the world. Secondly, he worked at the archives as usual, those at Dublin Castle. The archives at the Four Courts, so important for the legal institutions and records, were destroyed in our time in the civil war between the two Irish factions, republicans against the Free State, in which the traditional weapon of political assassination was resorted to among themselves.

We should not regard Froude's most controversial work, *The English in Ireland*, by itself alone. It was published in three volumes between 1872 and 1874.

Once more Froude was reacting, sometimes hotly, to contemporary events. Gladstone's Disestablishment of the Irish Church removed one of the pillars of the Anglo-Irish Ascendancy; his land legislation was to do the rest. Froude was in favour of this: gradually removing the hold of the landlords, aristocracy and gentry, and constituting a society of small farmers and peasant proprietors. Whether that meant an advance in civilisation and culture may be doubted, if that is to be the test of a society. The Irish scholar, Myles Dillon – son of the anti-English Home Rule leader – regarded it as 'the rule of the gombeen man'. My own standards remain, like Burckhardt's, determinedly aesthetic; they were not Froude's. His were moral.

The English in Ireland, which deals mainly with the 18th century, is then continuous with the long chapters on Irish history throughout the great History of England. Altogether, this constitutes a history of Ireland from Henry VIII's Reformation state to the Act of Union of 1801. I may as well get my own chief criticism off my chest at the outset. Froude had no appreciation of the cultural aspects of Anglo-Irish civilisation: he had more sympathy for Irish peasants; he had no sense of the beauty and elegance of Georgian Dublin, of the exquisite architecture of the country houses, even of palaces like Castletown, Russborough, Powerscourt, Carton, the Bishop-Earl of Bristol's palace on the cliffs outside Londonderry; the grandeur of Trinity College, the Dublin Custom House and the Four Courts; the nobility of the Provost's House at Trinity, or the distinction of the Archbishop's palace at Armagh. So many of these, beautiful in themselves, were nurseries of civilised life and culture: Coole, of Lady Gregory and Yeats; Moore Park of George Moore; Bowen's Court, of Elizabeth Bowen; Drishane, of Somerville and Ross; Kilteragh of Sir Horace Plunket. So many of these were burned down, or pulled down, in our own uncivilised time.

Froude was no aesthete. In this too he shows up as a Victorian; for the Victorians had little, or no, appreciation of superior Georgian architecture and taste.

The Normans conquered Ireland, as they conquered England; they were then absorbed into Celtic Ireland, as they were absorbed into Anglo-Saxon – or, I should put it, Anglo-Celtic England (for we must not overlook Wales and the West of the island). By the end of the Middle Ages such English representation as there was had lapsed back into a little area around Dublin and a few coast towns, which had never been founded by un-urban Celts. 'The English government, occupied with Scotland and France, had no leisure to maintain a powerful central authority'; we should add 'no means': we should always remember the restriction of England's resources, in coping with the other island, almost as large – and its unprofitability.

Up to Henry VIII's modernising of the state, England had mostly left the Irish to their own devices; though during the French war of 1523–4 Desmond entered into negotiations with the French to send an army to Munster. Here was a pointer to the future. Henry VII and Henry VIII had been content to leave Irish rule, such as it was, to the Kildare branch of the Fitzgeralds, one of the Norman families now gone native. A Kildare rebellion at the crisis of the Reformation in England gave Henry and Cromwell the opportunity to quash their power for good and all, and to begin on the almost hopeless task of modernising Irish government from Dublin.

Froude regarded the rebellion as 'the first in which an outbreak against England assumed the features of a war of religion, the first which the Pope was especially invited to bless, and the Catholic powers as such to assist. The features of it, on a narrow scale, were identical with those of the later risings.' They were propelled by race and religion, not yet by a sense of nationality, for an Irish nation did not exist, nor were there the makings of a nation-state among the Irish themselves. The island was divided into four provinces: Leinster, Munster, Connaught, Ulster, each with its separate history, the last intricately intermixed with the Scots Celts, their cousins, across the narrow waters. There was no national history, merely that of the separate provinces, with their respective Annals. Then there was Dublin, with its Scandinavian origins, as were those of other coast towns. How to make a modern nation-state out of that? It took centuries – and English resources, let alone patience, were never fully up to it: Froude does not allow for that.

Warfare, feuds, family murders were endemic among the septs and clans, encouraged by tanistry in the succession to the chieftainship, especially in Ulster where the O'Neils had a murderous record within the family. Ultimately Sean O'Neil came out on top from this early in Elizabeth's reign. Froude calls him 'an adulterous murderer', as he was. He was also a strong personality of considerable ability: the custom of tanistry usually accorded with the survival of the fittest to rule. The O'Neil, prince in Ulster, was as

much of an expansionist as the English; he asserted
O'Neil superiority over the O'Connells of Tyrconnell,
the sept of second importance, and proceeded to
invade Connaught. The Earl of Desmond, supreme in
Munster, opposed him, having no wish to see an
O'Neil king in Ireland. When, in 1570, the Desmonds
offered the lordship to the Pope, they were bitterly
surprised at his rejecting the poisoned chalice.

In the South the Desmond principality was opposed
by the Ormonds; the earls of this family, the Butlers,
though not always its younger scions, remained loyal
to the English connexion. They were cousins of Anne
Boleyn, and thus doubly favoured by Elizabeth I, who
would have preferred to leave the lead to them in
Ireland. They had the advantage of being a cultivated
Court family, who could also address fellow Irish
chieftains in their own tongue. What a kettle of fish
Ireland was! Froude speaks of its 'usual appetite for
disorder', and regarded the Brehon customary code as
a blue-print for anarchy; even a Spanish report reg-
istered that the Irish were lazy and did not like work.

The immense superiorities and privileges of the
native chieftains, princely in the cases of O'Neil and
Desmond, bore hardly on lesser clans, both chiefs and
clansmen, let alone tenantry where they existed. They
would have done better under English rule, if only it
could be made effective. But that was the problem: it
meant suppressing the princes, and that was too
expensive. Besides race and religion held the clansmen to their native chiefs, however much they had to
put up with from their exorbitant claims and extor-
tions. Elizabethan government tried the remedy of
erecting Presidencies in the provinces, over and above

the chiefs; after the Desmond Rebellion in the 1580's, much of Munster was devastated, some of it open to confiscation, and hence colonisation. After the ultimate suppression of Ulster resistance at the end of Elizabeth's reign, it was James I who brought in the Presbyterian Scots to colonise the North.

As usual, Froude was unfair to Elizabeth I for all the worry Ireland gave her and her constant desire for order, for peace and quiet among irrational humans. 'An unsuccessful public servant never failed to find a friend in Elizabeth, whose disposition to quarrel with her ministers was usually in proportion to their ability.' Unfair, and quite untrue. Froude saw that 'the religious cry and the land cry fell in together.' 'The suppression of the Catholic services, enforced wherever the English had power [this was only in some portions of the country] created a weight of animosity which no other measure could have produced, and alone, perhaps, made the problem of Irish administration insoluble.' This is an interesting admission from him; in the event the Counter-Reformation won in Ireland, as it won in Poland – not dissimilar in their lack of centricity and discipline.

All the English reports on conditions agreed: Sidney, Tremayne,[1] Spenser: the Elizabethans were shocked at the disorder of a pre-medieval society, not settled but nomadic, living off its herds of cattle. What they envisaged was a settled state of counties and parishes, each with its squire and parson to keep order in the nursery, villages and village-life, farms

---

1. Froude knew his fellow Devonshireman's family perfectly well, but calls Edmund Tremayne 'Edward'.

and orchards, an obedient tenantry. What a dream! Hundreds of good folk spent their lives in these efforts, and found only their graves.

A group of West Country gentry, St Legers and Grenvilles, made a combined effort to take up confiscated lands around Cork: Froude is surprisingly unfavourable to them. Another Devonshireman, Sir Peter Carew, a typical Tudor adventurer, revived the long-dormant claims of his Norman ancestors to lands in the South. I much doubt Froude's exaggerated account of atrocities committed by Carew, though no doubt lives were lost on both sides. Froude's comment on his fellow Devonshireman's adventure is that 'Carew's covetousness had exploded the mine at once prematurely and in the most unfortunate direction; and he and his companions were compelled to suspend their ambition, and to wait till the law had decided in their favour before taking armed possession of other men's properties.' Actually, Carew had employed the antiquarian lawyer, John Hooker, to search for and verify the medieval title-deeds to the lands – the practical point was that the Middle Ages were over. Froude himself suggests that the chiefs who would not cultivate their land can hardly claim an absolute right to them.

An Anglo-Irish report said that 'the real cause of the mischief was the Devil, who would not have Ireland reformed.' Froude comments, 'but the land question, with the vindictive and ferocious attitude assumed by the English soldiers towards the people, was of considerable moment in furthering the Devil's purposes. . . . The English nation was shuddering over the atrocities of the Duke of Alva. Yet Alva's bloody sword never touched the young, the defenceless, or those whose sex even dogs can recognise and respect.' This is rhetoric: at the lowest estimate Alva put to death 9,000 people in the Netherlands, at the highest 18,000. Such was human conduct in the 16th century: has the record of the 20th been any better?

The primitive conditions in Ireland, and the savagery on both sides, drove some men mad. When he comes to a neurotic temperament like Humphry Gilbert's, who believed that only fear would reduce the wilder Irish to order, Froude condemns him out of hand. 'The Gilbert method of treatment has this disadvantage, that it must be carried out to the last extremity, or it ought not to be tried at all.' We might compare Hitler's extermination of the Jews in a supposedly civilised country in the 20th century; Gilbert's policy of terror was applied in war conditions four hundred years ago. Froude went on to make a stark indictment, not the less surprising for its being of a Devonshireman, and a famous Elizabethan seaman. Froude tells us that 'there were Protestants in Galway, and it is creditable to the native Irish that they did not revenge their own treatment upon them.'

These sentiments do not strike one as anti-Irish: they sound more anti-English. The fact was that Froude castigated both sides, the English more severely for what he regarded as their mis-government. What he disliked was the alternation of neglect with repression, the dreary cycle of easy-going conciliation, which led to rebellion, which then had to be suppressed or the whole country would be in flames, while England herself was in danger from foreign enemies. Froude was a simple either-or man; what he approved was the unique achievement of British rule in India.

When we come to his main work on the subject, *The English in Ireland*, he reveals more of his governing principles. In his long 'Preliminary' considerations he gets down to bed-rock: 'All societies of men are, in the nature of things, forced into relation with other societies of men.' – And 'What constitutes a nation? The right of a people to self-government consists and can consist in nothing but their power to defend themselves.' Edward I failed in his attempt to force the Scots into submission; Froude admired the Scots for this. Now, if only the Irish had fought like the Scots . . . but they had always been divided. They were not a nation.

This was a dangerous argument, and very unwelcome to Victorian ears. It was an assertion that power was what mattered, a naked appeal to force. It was more Germanic than English, more like Bismarck than Mr Gladstone. But Froude went on to spell it out in moral terms, not just crude 'blood and iron'. 'A natural right to liberty, irrespective of the ability to defend it, exists in nations as much as, and no more than, it exists in individuals.' He held that 'the superior part has a natural right to govern, the inferior part has a natural right to be governed. . . . The rights of man – if such rights there be – are not to liberty, but to wise direction and control.'

This is teaching still more unwelcome today, but we can see its relevance when we look around the world at the appalling spectacles presented by Uganda, or the Sudan, Nigeria or any of the black African states; or at the shambles of central America; even India is not what it was.

Perhaps Froude could have put his point more convincingly if he had made capacity for self-government as the proper test of independence. A reading of history would suggest that when a people or, rather, its upper classes, arrive at a sufficient degree of maturity to govern themselves, then their independence should be recognised. This was the lesson of the American War of Independence, which should never have been waged: the Colonies were of an age to govern themselves.

When was this point arrived at in Ireland?

The Anglo-Irish thought that Britain's defeat in the American Revolutionary war proved the case for themselves, and that the Constitution of 1782, forced upon Britain in the circumstances of defeat, had achieved it. *Their* Ireland would have been independent, with only the Crown as link. This was altogether too simple and optimistic a view, for they themselves, the Protestant Ascendancy, were a small minority in a largely Catholic country. They would shortly be overwhelmed by the majority. Even the Protestants of the North, dour Presbyterian farmers and manufacturing folk in Belfast, were not friendly to the grand gentry of the Parliament House in Dublin, admired orators like the dubious Flood (so suitably named) or the voluble Grattan.

As for the exclusion of the Catholic Irish from participation in power, we must remember that Catholics in England were similarly excluded, along with Jews, while the Presbyterians in Ulster had no share in power either. Government was a monopoly of the Anglican Anglo-Irish, and Froude stated specifically that the Church of England was not suited to Ireland or the Irish temperament.

What Froude constantly inveighs against throughout his book is what he calls the misgovernment of
Ireland. I cannot but think he exaggerates. There were
times when conditions were bad: society in England
itself was a subsistence society and conditions were
hard; when there was a bad harvest people starved. In
Ireland conditions were at their worst during periods of
instability and rebellion – during the appalling Nine
Years' War following upon the Massacre of 1641,
which wrought such ruin in the Protestant North,
enraged their fellow Puritans in England, and determined them to reconquer Ireland. When there was
stability, as under the stern authoritarian rule of
Strafford, conditions improved. Froude gave little or
no credit to the brighter intervals, when conditions
were better. Strafford's Bishop of Derry, Bishop
Bramhall, is described as just 'Laud's creature'. He was
a distinguished and deserving man, of the hightest
intellectual and moral calibre. Driven out of Ireland,
he returned at the Restoration as Archbishop of
Armagh and won good opinions for his steady moderation.

One cannot call Froude a perfectionist but, a
moralist, he certainly expected too much of ordinary
human nature. He inveighs against the corruption of
the 18th century Ascendancy in Dublin; was government in London any better? It is the nature of
aristocratic birds to feather their nests – but they at
least built beautifully from the proceeds. And not
aristocrats only – look at the corruption around
President Harding and Teapot Dome, or around Joe
Kennedy and over American party funds. But what have
they built? Froude had the exceptional standards of the

Victorian middle class, which he applied to all sorts and conditions of men – most hardly on the English, I suppose, because he expected the best of them.

Throughout the period Froude dealt with, the Irish could provide no stable basis of government for themselves. During the Nine Years' war in the middle of the 17th century, the native Irish were divided between the ultramontane Papal party and the loyal Royalist party under Ormond. The Papal legate Rinuccini had no sense of moderation, insisted on extreme Papal claims, and would not pull together with Ormond to defeat the English Puritans. So they both lost out, and the Puritans won with Oliver Cromwell. (Who was to blame for that?) At the Restoration a sympathetic Charles II restored a third of the lands confiscated by Cromwell for rebellion and massacre.

Meanwhile the strategic consideration retained its dominance. At the Revolution of 1688 the Catholic Irish rallied to James II, who returned with a French army to reverse his brother, Charles II's settlement – and to lose the battle of the Boyne to his nephew and son-in-law, William III. There followed a century of stability and peace under the Anglo-Irish Ascendancy: no more rebellions. There were Penal Laws against the Catholics, but they were largely inoperative. Catholicism remained the religion of the majority, Presbyterianism (though unprivileged) in Ulster.

Where Froude is right is in his damning indictment of England for frustrating the prospects of the Protestant interest and its own colonial offshoot. After the Restoration the English landed interest refused to allow the import of Irish cattle, a discouraging restriction, against the more generous and far-sighted wishes

of Charles II and Clarendon. Strafford had encouraged
the linen industry in Ulster; in the South the 'great
Earl of Cork' developed some industry, as Sir William
Petty did later in Kerry. But English self-interest laid a
prohibition on Irish woollens, in the hands of Protestant manufacturers and craftsmen. This is the gravamen of Swift's charges: the economic self-interest of
the English stifled the development and increase of
their own Protestant establishment in Ireland. Froude
was in agreement with Swift.

A further indictment was on the score of absenteeism among the greater landlords. There was a distinguished society in Georgian Dublin, of which ocular
evidences remain in the slums of ruined Mountjoy
Square, or famous Merrion Square. But as com-
munications improved, so did absenteeism increase,
even more so in the 19th century. Froude quotes at
length the indictment made by a Georgian viceroy:
'Were the country gentlemen – or, rather, were the
great landed proprietors – to reside on their estates,
were the parochial clergy more numerous or more
generally resident; were the gentlemen more active,
the provincial magistracy better filled, the duties of it
discharged with impartiality and the police establishment made general through Ireland; were the wages of
the labourers better regulated and paid in specie; and
the lands so occupied as to give the landlord an
influence over the farmer and the farmer an interest in
the good-will of the proprietor of the estate – then
much might be done for the improvement of the
kingdom and the happiness of its inhabitants.'

Such were the aims and good intentions of English
administration at its best – constantly defeated of

course by the facts of human nature, Irish or otherwise
– and Froude never gave English government in
Ireland any credit for these. Instead, he savaged it in
his analysis of 'Four methods of administering the
government of a dependent country: the method
adopted in Ireland the worst.' Too extreme, too
immoderate – as the historian Lecky complained in
the weightiest criticism the book received. The moralist in Froude was more interested in high-lighting what
he considered 'the secret of all Ireland's disorders: the
scandalous forgetfulness of duty on the part of every
person in the empire connected with the management
of it – from the sovereign who had quartered his
mistresses[1] on the Irish revenue to the lowest customs
officer, who contrived to be sick in his bed when the
Kerry smuggler landed his cargo.' But this was to omit
the Irish people.

Froude would have done better to follow the more
sceptical motto of Pope, quoted by an Anglo-Irish
politician:

For modes of government let fools contest:
Whate'er is best administered is best.

Such was the motto of the sceptical Boies Penrose,
who ruled the Republican Party in the United States,
before the idealism of Woodrow Wilson took over –
and crashed.

1. This is a dig at the Hanoverian George I's mistress (he had
   brought two over to England), the greedy German Ehrengard
   Melusina von der Schulenburg, whom he made Duchess of
   Kendal. The *D.N.B.* gives her mistakenly to George II, who
   had a good English mistress.

In fact Ireland made progress under Georgian stability and achieved a modicum of prosperity, so far as the poverty of the soil allowed, so much of it mountain and bog. Then at the end all was upset again by the revolutionary spirit let loose by the French Revolution, which spread over Western Europe and threatened Britain itself. Irish malcontents, a small minority, headed by such reckless types as Wolfe Tone and the irresponsible aristocrat, Lord Edward Fitzgerald, took the opportunity to cash in on it and instigate revolution in Ireland. Republican spirit was at its most vehement in Ulster, and Wolfe Tone put his shirt, or staked his life, on bringing together Protestant Ulstermen with Southern Catholics in the United Irishmen of 1797. Some hopes!

However, his hopes were high, for in this year Britain was in mortal danger from the Mutiny at the Nore, her coasts uncovered by her wooden bulwarks to the threat from France. Tone hoped to co-ordinate rebellion in Ireland with a French invasion, and helped to plan it with the Revolutionary General Hoche. A large French fleet, with a considerable army of some 7000, left Brest for Bantry Bay. If they had landed it would have been dangerous for Britain, as at several previous crises in relation to Ireland during wars with France and Spain. Happily bad weather came to the rescue: the fleet was dispersed, the army returned to France; only separate detachments subsequently landed to intervene, when savage rebellion broke out in Wexford in 1798.

Again it was not a national, but partial, outbreak: the Ulster Presbyterians, for all their republican discontent, would never co-operate with the Catholic

South. 'United Irishmen' was a dream. The Rebellion
of 1798 was, however, a savage affair and savagely
repressed, for England was in danger and in no mood
for half-measures. Strategic necessity had once more
taken over.

As a consequence, some of the best brains in Britain
and Ireland – and with the best intentions – decided
on Union with Britain as a solution for the problem of
Ireland. The Union with Scotland from 1707 had
been an historic success; actually at that time a
proposal for Union was made from Ireland and
(perhaps unwisely) not taken up. Such a Union, in
19th century circumstances, with increasing religious
toleration and gradual freeing of the sects from disabil-
ities, would need to be fulfilled by Catholic Eman-
cipation. This, as so often had happened in Irish
history, was postponed until too late.

Would it have made any difference?

Only once, in the course of Froude's long history,
though I may be doing him an injustice, does the veil
drop from his eyes, and he saw, what the wise Lord
Derby told him, that one free democratic country
cannot rule another. Only an empire can – as the
Russians, the imperialists today, take on Afghanistan.
And once again, in a moment of truth, Froude
admitted that the fundamental wish of the Irish
population was to see the English out.

However, whatever the historical pros and cons of
Froude's book, and it was more widely attacked than
any other (oddly enough the American historian,
Bancroft, heartily approved of it), he certainly made
the last volume of it as exciting as a novel.

History and Literature

Historical writing is a most important part of literature, though this is hardly realised in the over-
specialisation and the lowering of cultural standards
today. Specialised historians are apt to be ill-read in
literature: they show it in their writing; literary people
are insufficiently read in history and fail to realise that
literature is the prime expression of a society, the
history of which is a necessity for fully understanding
its literature. (This failing is particularly noticeable in
a purely literary approach to Shakespeare's work, the
richest reflection of the Elizabethan age, which in turn
contributed its richness to the work.)

The point needs no arguing. Where would Greek
literature be without Herodotus or Thucydides; or
Latin literature without Caesar, Tacitus, Livy or
Suetonius? All great historians have contributed significantly to literature – Clarendon, Gibbon, Hume; in
the 19th century Macaulay and Froude no less than
their contemporaries in France, Michelet and Renan.
In addition to their historical work as such, in itself an
addition to literature, both Macaulay and Froude
disported themselves with purely, or mixed, literary
writing. Here we must concentrate on the historical
aspect.

In 1879, taking a rest from his long labours on

English history, Froude produced his biography of Julius Caesar. He called it 'A Sketch', 'because the materials do not exist for a portrait which shall be at once authentic and complete.' However, it is a full-length biography, and was a favourite with him among his works. Indeed, it needs no apology. Froude was educated in the classics; his reading for preference was Greek, especially the *Odyssey*, Euripides and Pindar. He cites all the authorities he consulted for Caesar's life; they can hardly have been significantly added to in our time, except possibly for archaeological discoveries and inscriptions. Froude had read the leading authority in his own time, Mommsen, for at one point he registers a modest score against the monster target.

I am not qualified to make an authoritative judgment, not being a Roman historian. I can only say that it is the most vivid and readable biography of Caesar of several that I have read, and when I compare it with the up-to-date scholarship of the *Cambridge Ancient History* I do not find Froude wide of the mark. Naturally he is more sympathetic to Caesar than the leading Roman historian of our time, A.H.M. Jones, with his Leftist sympathies, who could not forgive Caesar for the fall of the Republic, though the Republic was already falling of itself anyway. Once more we catch a reaction to Froude's own time (as with Gibbon's *Decline and Fall of the Roman Empire*) when he points out that consultative assemblies, subject to party dispute and division, are not capable of ruling an empire. *Verb. sap.*

I do not need to bring home to the reader the vividness of Froude's reconstruction of life in ancient Rome: it is all there in a phrase, 'to be murdered was the usual end of exceptionally distinguished Romans.' The combined savagery and culture, the brutality and intellectual enlightenment, are evoked as convincingly as today in Montherlant's classical *La Guerre Civile*, another product of education in the classics. Again there is the visual gift of genius. In ordinary social life one is constantly struck by how few people can ever describe another person's appearance. Not so Froude: here is Caesar to the life. 'In person Caesar was tall and slight. His features were more refined than was usual in Roman faces; the forehead was wide and high, the nose large and thin, the lips full, the eyes dark grey like an eagle's, the neck extremely thick and sinewy. His complexion was pale. His beard and moustache were kept carefully shaved. His hair was short and naturally scanty, falling off towards the end of his life and leaving him partially bald. His voice, especially when he spoke in public, was high and shrill.' Froude then goes on to his characteristics.

We must confine ourselves to what reveals the historian. 'Men of genius are governed by their instinct; they follow where instinct leads them; and the public life of a nation is but the life of successive generations of statesmen, whose horizon is bounded, and who act from day to day, as immediate interests suggest.' Common sense tells us, and political observation confirms it, that this is true. Thus, 'irrespective of the direct teaching which we may gather from them, particular epochs in history have the charm for us which dramas have – periods when the great actors on the stage of life stand before us with the distinctiveness with which they appear in the creations of a poet.'

The appeal of history to Froude was double – both

moral and dramatic (as with Shakespeare); we might say that it was also poetic, evocative, nostalgic. In short, it was life on the page, not something dead and done with. Dull periods and subjects might be left to the dull historian. 'But there are others, a few, at which intellectual activity was as great as it is now, with its written records surviving, in which the passions, the opinions, the ambitions of the age are all before us; where the actors in the great drama speak their own thoughts in their own words. . . .' We note again his creditable addiction to citing contemporary records and documents, statutes, speeches, letters: the evidence upon which we can make up our own minds, if we have minds to make up.

We note again Froude's reaction to his own time. 'Notwithstanding many differences, the English and the Romans essentially resemble one another. The early Romans possessed the faculty of self-government beyond any people of whom we have historical knowledge, with the one exception of ourselves.' He saw the age of Cato and Pompey, of Cicero and Julius Caesar as 'in so many ways the counterpart of our own, the blossoming point of the old civilisation. . . .' No-one can dispute the primacy of the Victorian age in English civilisation, the creative richness of its culture in so many fields – science, industry, technology, medicine no less. However, on the political plane, Froude drew the familiar moral: 'if there be one lesson which history clearly teaches, it is this – that free nations cannot govern subject provinces.'

On a deeper level we may read the lesson of the element of inevitability there is in history. People agitate for a change of government, dispute about a change of system, conspire and combine for revolt and revolution. 'They imagine that they see what the change should be, that they comprehend what they are doing, and know where they intend to arrive. They do not perceive that the visible disorders are no more than symptoms which no measures, repressive or revolutionary, can do more than palliate. The wave advances and the wave recedes. Neither party in the struggle can lift itself far enough above the passions of the moment to study the drift of the general current.'

At the same time those who think they know how things will turn out are almost always caught out. In an essay Froude pointed out that one can never predict from history; Gibbon wrote out of the complacency of the Augustan age expecting an era of peace and tranquillity: he himself had to run from the French Revolution. Macaulay wrote out of the optimism of the early Victorian age expecting a century of peace and progress: there followed a century of wars. And progress? Froude wrote a Short Study on the subject. 'Amidst the varied reflections which the 19th century is in the habit of making on its condition and its prospects, there is one common opinion in which all parties coincide – that we live in an era of progress.'

He subjected the concept to his usual scrutiny without Victorian illusions. In *Caesar* he wrote of that age – he must have been reading Cicero, for whom he had no high opinion: 'the whole spiritual atmosphere was saturated with cant – cant moral, cant political, cant religious; an affectation of high principle which had ceased to touch the conduct, and flowed on in an increasing volume of insincere and unreal speech. The truest thinkers were those who, like Lucretius, spoke

frankly out their real convictions and declared that
Providence was a dream.' This was fairly clearly what
Froude thought of the Victorian age; he might well
have subscribed to what one of its last Liberals
declared: 'the longer I live the more I see that things
really are as silly as they seem.'

I think that this is what upset Victorians about
Froude, not exactly irony, not precisely Arnold's
persiflage, but the cold eye he cast upon their illusions,
for he had no cant.

Naturally one can pick holes in *Caesar*. Froude
accepts Caesar's numbers of the Gauls he encountered
in battle. I have never been able to accept them; I am
sure that the colossal numbers he gives are much
exaggerated. I find them incredible, but, curiously
enough, I have not been able to persuade Roman
historians of this. An important point in historiography arises here: nearly all historians exaggerate numbers, not only ancient writers like those of the Old
Testament; *all* medievals exaggerate numbers. John
Wesley often wrote of audiences of thousands that
came to hear him, when it was more credibly hundreds.

Again, Froude takes the trouble to defend Caesar
against the charge of sexual ambivalence. A contemporary Roman historian, with the candour of today,
tells us that heterosexuality, at least exclusively, was 'a
rare phenomenon among Roman rulers'.[1] It is curious
that, when homosexuality was so common, it should
so often have been made a charge against eminent
persons. We should regard it as another example of

1. Michael Grant, *The Roman Emperors*, 33.

human cant. Froude defends his hero: 'the disposition to believe evil of men who have risen a few degrees above their contemporaries is a feature of human nature as common as it is base.' True enough: James Anthony Froude was very high-minded, but also, I fear, rather a prude.

The following year he published a pleasant little book on the uncongenial Bunyan – the family name must derive from 'bunnion' – whose vogue was at its height in the Nonconformist world of the 19th century. Its interest for us must lie in Froude's view of the 17th century. Puritans 'not only believed that God had miraculously governed the Israelites, but they believed that as directly and immediately He governed England in the 17th century' (more fools they). 'They not only believed that there had been a witch at Endor, but they believed that there were witches in their own villages, who had made compacts with the Devil himself.' Hence the appalling persecution of old crones, the hangings of scores (if not a couple of hundred), when the Puritans gained control in the Civil War; there had been no witch-mania under the civilised Charles I and Laud.

Increasing years seem to have lessened Froude's incomprehensible admiration for Calvinism. 'Horror at sin forces the sinner to confess it, and makes others eager to punish it.' The uncivilised Puritans passed an act of Parliament to punish adultery with death. One of the leading Parliament men, Sir Henry Marten, was a notorious adulterer. Cant again. All over the country the ungenial hypocrites campaigned against the King's *Book of Sports*, allowing one day of recreation in the week in the labourers' hard-worked lives: in 1644

Parliament banned the book. Froude writes: 'but the gloom of a Presbyterian Sunday was, is, and for ever will be detestable to the natural man.'

'Powerful temperaments are necessarily intense.' Bunyan, like St Teresa of Avila, about whom Froude wrote with even more sympathy, combined neurotic and hysterical symptoms with some practicality and common sense. 'He saw evil spirits in monstrous shapes and fiends blowing flames out of their nostrils': material for his subsequent popular works. He became a much admired preacher, though 'the excitement of perpetual speech-making is fatal to the exercise of the higher qualities'. Bunyan's best book was written in Bedford Gaol, when preaching was suspended: evidently a good idea to keep him there.

Froude tells us that *The Life and Death of Mr Badman* 'contains a vivid picture of rough English life in the days of Charles II': useful social history then. But we need not agree that Bunyan's doctrine was the doctrine of the best and strongest minds in Europe', because it was that of Luther and John Knox and Oliver Cromwell. They were activists, who made life a battlefield. The best minds thought otherwise: Erasmus and Grotius, prophets of international peace and toleration; or in England, Bacon and his brilliant amanuensis, Hobbes, who thought humans the fools they all too often show themselves to be.

Froude disagreed with Macaulay's view that 'if there had been no *Pilgrim's Progress*, *The Holy War* would have been the first of religious allegories. We may admire the workmanship, but the same undefined sense of unreality which pursues us through Milton's epic would have interfered equally with the accept-

ance of this.' Froude regarded *Paradise Lost* as unsatis-
factory as an epic: 'Milton himself had not arrived at
thinking it to be a legend, a fiction like the Greek
mythology.' The author of *Paradise Lost* was 'only
partially emancipated from the bondage of the letter
. . . his poem falls between two modes of treatment
and two conceptions of truth.' We see that Froude was
not a blinkered Protestant in his tastes; he was too
good a writer: he preferred Greek to Christian mythology. He considered that 'the religious history of man is
essentially the same in all ages': properly the subject
for anthropology.

Froude concluded: 'if the "Holy War" is an unfit
subject for allegorical treatment, the "Pilgrim's Progress" is no less perfectly adapted for it.' He had a due
appreciation of the book – I concede it is a classic: 'dear
to all men of all creeds . . . who continue to see in
conscience an authority for which culture is no substi-
tute . . . even though it pleases the "elect" modern
philosophers to describe its author as a "Philistine of
genius".' This was Matthew Arnold, of course.

Froude was occupied in the 1880's mainly with the
work that had been wished on him by Carlyle, dealing
with the large mass of papers which were his *Nachlass*,
editing his *Reminiscences*, then the Letters and Memo-
rials of Mrs Carlyle, finally writing the big biography.
It is usual to regard this as one of the three chief
literary biographies in the language, along with Bos-
well's Johnson and Lockhart's Scott. We can hardly
place it in the same class with those, if only that the
subject of it is not in the same class as Dr Johnson or
Sir Walter Scott. Further, it is too long and too
diffuse. Froude wonders in his Preface whether it is not

to be regarded as Materials for a Life. It certainly quotes far too much of Carlyle's endless and wearisome outpourings, from his Journals, of self-pity and his woes, his stomach-aches and sleeplessness, his dyspeptic view of the world and everybody.

It is difficult for us today to appreciate the primacy which was accorded to Carlyle in Victorian literary life. That is not our subject, though we can view the biography historically as a partial portrait of the age. For Carlyle was a considerable pivot, around whom much centered. Sooner or later everybody turned up at Cheyne Row – Tennyson, Ruskin, John Stuart Mill, Caroline Fox, Emerson, Louis Blanc, Louis Napoleon, Mazzini; before this Carlyle had made the acquaintance of the *Edinburgh Review* circle; and of Coleridge and Lamb; he was in correspondence with Goethe.

Nor can we go into detail why and how he achieved this ascendancy, partly the originality of his genius and characteristics. A Scotch peasant, he happened to be better educated than most of his rival intellectuals, well read not only in the classics but in French, Spanish, Italian, above all German. The last was something new. Here he was on a moving escalator, with Germany and everything German coming to the fore in the 19th century: in scholarship, philosophy, music, science and technology, and, alas, in power and politics. Then, too, a man of the people, Carlyle had no middle-class illusions about them. In one way his sympathies were with them, and he brought 'the Condition of England' question to the notice of his time. G.M. Trevelyan used to divide Carlyle into two halves: the early Carlyle with his warm-hearted, Radical sympathies, and the later, dusty and disillusioned, having lost belief in his own message, with a despairing outlook on the world and nothing more to say to it. He always was, as Froude says, 'a Calvinist without the theology'; he had no Christian belief, any more than Froude had.

One other consideration. The historian, Sir Charles Oman, once told me that, in our time, we could have no conception of the pedestals upon which the Victorians placed the eminences of theirs. They were expected to be without reproach, and their biographies in keeping. We can see something of this in the flummery of the official biographies of the Prince Consort or the (far from irreproachable) Edward VII; even more in Hallam Tennyson's biography of his father, the poet laureate, emptied of all interest, without flesh or blood, a whited sepulchre. This has been put right in our time by Tennyson's grandson telling us the full story, the incredible Brontesque background with its neurosis, madness and genius, at last revealing the exceptional man Tennyson really was.

It was the historian in Froude that made him portray Carlyle as he was, warts and all. And it raised a huge scandal, the largest amount of controversy Froude encountered over any of his books, which overshadowed and embittered the last years of his life, so that on his death-bed he adjured his daughter Margaret to destroy all his letters and papers. As we have seen she did not carry this out fully. It made one of the most famous literary rows there have ever been, extending itself even to America, where the celebrated Harvard professor, Charles Eliot Norton, played a leading hand. It stimulated an extensive literature, all of which I have read in my time. I do not propose to go into it, any more than into the personal vendetta with which the cantankerous Freeman pursued Froude.

My own opinion is that Froude did Carlyle more than justice – far more than Carlyle did his equals. Though generous enough in personal affairs, charitable to the poor etc, Carlyle could never bring himself to be generous about other writers, his contemporaries. He cuts them all down to less than size, Coleridge, Lamb, John Stuart Mill, Newman, Emerson, to whom he owed so much for fostering his reputation, and protecting his copyrights, in America. Froude wrote, 'when the Devil's advocate has said his worst against Carlyle, he leaves a figure still of unblemished integrity, purity, loftiness of purpose, and inflexible resolution to do right.'

Pure, Carlyle certainly was, for he was practically impotent. His marriage with Jane Welsh was a *marriage blanche*. She said later that she had married him out of ambition; he had fulfilled her wildest hopes, and 'I am miserable'. She might have married Edward Irving,[1] who was in love with her and could have given her what she wanted. Later on, when Carlyle's head was turned by the grand Lady Ashburton, Mrs Carlyle felt deeply aggrieved: if she could not have his body, at least she should have sole possession of his soul.

A crucial fact in the controversy is that Froude knew this secret, but did not wish to divulge it. Carlyle himself gave a clue when he said that 'no one was likely to understand a history, the secret of which

1. Founder of the 'Catholic Apostolic' Church, a typical piece of Victorian nonsense.

was unknown to his closest friends'. But there were
other intimates of the household who knew, or guessed, what was what. What was Froude to do? A
discreet principle for an historian in these matters is to
write in such a way that those who do understand will
understand, and those who don't won't. Once more
Froude was attacked for – what is the word for it? –
disingenuousness; his enemies, crudely and unsubtly,
called it lying. Tennyson had the last word on the
Carlyle marriage; he said that he was in favour of it: it
meant that only two people were unhappy, instead of
four.

We need remark only on the historical importance
of Carlyle's career, with which Froude sympathised.
They were both unreconstructed Teutonists. Carlyle
devoted thirteen years of his life to his *Frederick the
Great* in many volumes; it received enormous acclaim
in Germany, since it ministered to German self-
esteem and spread wide praise of the remarkable
Frederick. (Did Carlyle realise that his Friedrich was a
well-known homosexual? I have no prejudice in the
matter, only it is an important element in understanding Frederick the Great.[1] To omit it is either ignor-
ance or humbug.) Carlyle's lengthy hymn of praise for
Frederick, or, rather his epic, gained him the Prussian
Ordre pour le Mérite, which he accepted, though he
refused to accept any English honour. The book was
Hitler's reading in his last days.

For all the denigration Froude's *Carlyle* received,
judicious minds knew better. The scholarly Lord
Derby wrote: 'you have written the most interesting

1.   cf. my *Homosexuals in History*.

biography in the English language. It is clear to me that you have done only, and exactly, what Carlyle wished done; and to me it is also apparent that he and you were right – that his character could not have been understood without a full disclosure of what was least attractive in it.'

That was no more than a historian's duty, as Froude understood and practised it.

A little book which he was invited to write on *Beaconsfield* (1890) adds a few strokes to his depiction of his own time. Neither Carlyle nor Froude much cared for Gladstone or Disraeli, its two polarising figures in politics. To his pro-Germanism Carlyle added a strain of anti-Jewish feeling, the last ignoble infirmity of any mind. Froude was above that, and was a friend of the Rothschilds. The sheer romance of Disraeli's career appealed to him, and Dizzy romanticised his own Jewish descent. He had conquered Parliament, had made his ascent through Parliament, but he never talked democratic platitudes. 'For cant of all kinds he had the natural hatred which belongs to real ability. The Rights of Man to what was called Liberty he never meddled with. He desired practical results.'

Something more personal may have drawn Froude to him. From the first Disraeli had known his own quality, and was unpopular at school. 'Superiority begets jealousy. Boys never pardon a comrade who is unlike themselves' – the bores. As a boy Disraeli had been taken away from school: Froude must have remembered that he had had to be taken away from Westminster. He quoted Swift: 'the appearance of a man of genius in the world may be always known by the virulence of dunces'. Froude admired Disraeli's writing, the brilliance of his letters, and especially his late novel *Lothair*, with its portrait of Victorian society and the fuss it made over Catholic converts like the Butes and Cardinal Manning – the novel was a *roman à clef*.

In politics Disraeli was often odd man out, too original to be conventional. As a famous old man he said endearingly to the obstreperous Lord Randolph Churchill, 'I was never very respectable myself as a young man.' He had been sympathetic to the Chartists: in effect he was a Tory Radical (Froude might be regarded as such), and described the Conservative Party as 'an organised hypocrisy'. He then proceeded to reorganise it.

He had, however, always been pro-Turk. Over the conflict in the Middle East between Russia and Turkey, Froude was pro-Russian. He thought the Crimean War a mistake, and quoted Cobden's view that 'if Disraeli and Lord Derby had not been turned out of office in 1852 they would have prevented it, and a million lives and a hundred million of English money need not have been sacrificed over a struggle which events proved to be useless. . . . We drifted into a war of which the only direct result was a waste of money which, if wisely used, might have drained the Bog of Allen, turned the marshes of the Shannon into pasture ground, and have left in Ireland some traces of English rule to which we could look with satisfaction.' Disraeli never touched the hot potato of the Irish Question; Gladstone raised it as a party card.

When a further advance of Russian expansionism resulted in the war of 1877–8 with Turkey, Froude

aligned himself with Gladstone. He even appeared on
the same platform with Professor Freeman, who, as a
Liberal was of course anti-Turk. Froude was definitely
pro-Russian: 'The world smiles when we complain of
Russian aggression. The Asiatic subjects of the Queen
of England are 200 millions. The Asiatic subjects of
Russia are 40 millions. [Things are different now!]
The right on both sides is the right of conquest.'
Victorians did not like that sort of talk, or to have the
facts of life brought home to them so rawly. The
historian recognised that all vigorous societies
expand, decadent societies contract. Perhaps he was
unfair to Disraeli, who at least kept the Russians out
of Constantinople.

Over Anglo-Russian relations Froude was again in
hot water. Some people thought him too pro-Russian,
others not sufficiently ardent. He was accused of being
under the influence of the Russian agent, Mme Novi-
kov. In the controversy that ensued he eventually
cleared himself of the charge of undue influence and
proved that he had a clear record. I do not fully
understand what it was that provoked people to attack
him so much. He delayed in explaining his precise
relations with the Russophile lady, and his defence of
his great biography, My Relations with Carlyle, did not
appear until after his death. It is obvious that ordinary
people could not make him out; but why should he
explain or defend himself to fools? It was for them at
least to try to understand.

The late 19th century was dominated by the colonial scramble for Africa. Here again Froude took an
independent line; he was called upon by the Colonial
Secretary, Lord Caernarvon, to go out, take a hand in

negotiations, and report.[1] Froude's intervention was quite unsuccessful, naturally: no-one could get it right, one could not square the circle any more than in Ireland. Once again controversy raised its boring head. Froude, whom we think of as an imperialist, was against the annexation of the Transvaal; he thought that the British had treated the Boers badly, as they had, and that these should be left alone.

'Sir Bartle Frere in South Africa imagined that he could have an Imperial policy. He went to war with the Kaffirs. He went to war with the Zulus, whom – if he had been wise – he would have helped and favoured as a check upon the ambition of the Boers [who were taking their lands on the disputed frontier of Natal]. Frere's policy was his own; Lord Beaconsfield was not responsible for it, and did not approve of it. Yet the war went on.' He did not intervene, but confined himself to phrase-making: when the Prince Imperial was killed there: 'A very remarkable people, the Zulus: they defeat our Generals, they convert our Bishops

1.   Froude published *Two Lectures on South Africa* in 1880: his contribution to its too interesting history. It is an uncompromising indictment of the British rôle in South Africa, alternating between disinterest and intervention. Froude's account is pro-Boer in sentiment, though he did not subscribe to the Boer attitude to the blacks: 'good treatment of the natives would be simply impossible under a Dominion two-thirds of which would be Dutch. . . . For myself, I would wait to establish a South African Dominion till the law should know no distinction of colour, and the black races can be enfranchised, as the slaves have been enfranchised in the Southern States of the American Union.' He paid tribute to Bishop Colenso's brave stand on behalf of the blacks.

[i.e. Colenso]; they have settled the fate of a great European dynasty' (Napoleon's).

Today we can subscribe to Froude's conclusion still. 'Perhaps no public man in England ever rose so high and acquired power so great, so little of whose work has survived him.' Still Disraeli is better remembered than many who wrought more – for good or ill. What is the explanation of the paradox? Like Froude himself, he had genius, and so was unaccountable.

Next year Froude produced a substantial work, *The Divorce of Catherine of Aragon*, which is, in effect, an appendix to his early volumes on Henry VIII. Since those, many of the State Papers from the archives at home and abroad had been printed. Though Froude had much to elaborate, he had little to correct, so much of his work had rested on the originals. This late work gives us his matured reflections on the nature of history and historical writing, after a lifetime of its practice. 'The mythic element cannot be eliminated out of history. Men's outward acts, being public, cannot be absolutely misstated; their motives, being known only to themselves [not always then!] are an open field for imagination. As the disposition is to believe evil rather than good, the portraits drawn may vary indefinitely, according to the sympathies of the describer, but are seldom too favourable.'

'People believe or disbelieve, repeat or suppress, according to their own inclinations' – one of the most tiresome things about them to a reflective mind, and a good reason for never taking their opinions seriously. Froude found that there was little of importance to correct in his early work – minor inaccuracies, of course, as with every historian. He still held by his portrait and his estimate of Henry VIII, but found that he was still alone in his opinion of him – naturally for people in general simply go by their likes and dislikes.

We find, from a letter to Carlyle, that Froude did now have doubts about the guilt of Anne Boleyn. He found the charges made of her attempting to poison Queen Catherine and intending to poison Princess Mary too incredible. But he found it difficult to get round extorted or misreported 'confessions' and the 'evidence' so assiduously compiled and put across the court by Cromwell. Froude lived in an age that had civilised upper-class standards: we know better today how these things could be arranged, in the People's courts of Nazi Germany or Soviet Russia.

Froude's early scepticism had come up again in his mind. 'To appreciate any single man with complete accuracy is impossible. To appreciate him even proximately is extremely difficult.' Still more with a woman: that should have given him some pause over Elizabeth I and her maligned mother. Froude allowed that Philip II was unduly maligned by Protestants, and that William the Silent's Manifesto was 'a libel' against him (however, Philip did instigate his assassination). Froude then went further in scepticism, by way of justifying the ethical value of history and its moral implications, than a modern historian, more literally strict to facts, would allow. 'The tendency of history is to fall into wholesome moral lines whether they be accurate or not, and to interfere with harmless illusions may cause greater errors than it aspires to cure.' That appears to me to show a paradox, if not a contradiction, in moralising history: with us the truth, and nothing but the truth is what matters to the elect,

111

leaving people to their futile illusions, by no means harmless, by the way. Perhaps this may appear a strict view, but truth, like art, is only for the elect.

At last this reserved man explained himself and gave an opinion of his own work. 'I myself, after reading and weighing all that I could find forty years ago in prints or manuscripts, concluded that the real facts of Henry's conduct were to be found in the Statute Book and nowhere else.' Froude found that 'the published criticisms upon my work were generally unfavourable.' As one might expect, Catholics and Protestants reacted – one cannot say 'judged' – in accordance with their prejudices, as did others with their preconceptions. 'The public, however, took an interest in what I had to say. The book was read, and continues to be read.' This was a modest statement of the case: in fact he was a best-seller, edition followed edition of his works: my copy of his *Beaconsfield* is a fifth edition the year after publication!

He noted how much that had been only partially accessible earlier had 'since been sorted, catalogued and calendared by the industry of my friends Mr Brewer and Mr Gairdner'; other workers had followed him in the private collections since then reported on by the Historical Manuscripts Commission. 'Foreign archives at Paris, Simancas, Rome, Venice, Vienna, and Brussels have been searched to some extent by myself, but in a far larger degree by able scholars specially appointed for the purpose.'

Then, 'Finally I do not allow myself to be tempted into controversy with particular writers whose views disagree with my own.' So much for Professor Freeman. 'My censors have been so many that a reply to them all is impossible, and so distinguished that a selection would be invidious' – one of those ironic touches that so nettled people.

Next year, 1892, he published a further appendage to the History in the shape of a volume of essays, 'carefully written', *The Spanish Story of the Armada, and Other Essays*: published in April, it was reprinted in June. He had intended to continue with the 16th century, and write the lives of Charles V and Philip II; from this he had been deflected by his decade of work on Carlyle. 'To regard the Emperor, to regard Philip merely as reactionary bigots [as Motley did] is as unjust as it is uninstructive.' The three main essays are considerable pieces from Froude's years of research into Spanish history, illuminated by his knowledge of Spain and the landscape.

It was a brilliant idea to present the story of the Armada of 1588 from the Spanish point of view. He had himself discovered at Simancas the narrative of the Accountant-General of the Fleet, Don Pedro Calderòn. This was now followed by Captain Duro's two volumes, *La Armada Invencible*, of original documents and letters. Froude's own seamanship, his intimate knowledge of sea and weather conditions in the Channel, of the coasts and also of the Irish coast upon which so many galleons were wrecked, make the story not only enthralling reading, but an invaluable contribution, much neglected today, to history.

He is admiring of, and generous about, the gallant and experienced sea-captains on board, several of whom perished in the *Empresa*. He is less than just to the poor Duke of Medina Sidonia, who was no seaman, did not want the job, but at least kept the fleet together as far as the Orkneys. But the Duke was as severely criticised by his own side, and stoned when he got back to Spain. Philip II did not reproach him for the fiasco; Froude contrasts this gentlemanly conduct with Elizabeth I's – once again unfairly: she did *not* starve her Navy, she did her best for it according to the resources available.

Froude's line on this has been adopted by all naval historians since, quite wrongly, and the general misestimation of Medina Sidonia, which became traditional, has been modified only today.[1] We should take seriously Froude's criticisms on seamanship, however. He thought that the Duke should have staked everything on gaining a port, a foothold on the coast, and forced his way into St Helen's. Off Calais, when the English fire-ships were launched against the Armada, 'the Duke, instead of sending launches to tow them clear, fired a signal for the whole fleet to get instantly under way', cutting their cables and getting dispersed, in imminent danger of being blown in on the shoals of the Flemish coast, if the wind had not changed and saved them.

A technical point may be made: the English guns were *not* heavier (the Spanish were), but of longer range, as we now know from the researches of gunnery-expert, Michael Lewis. Froude knew from experience the dangers of the west coast of Ireland, and gives a thrilling account of survivor Captain Cuellar's account of his adventures. His depiction of the primitive savagery of Irish conditions agreed with Elizabethan reports of them.

1.   cf. G. Mattingly, *The Defeat of the Spanish Armada.*

The essay on Antonio Pérez is entitled, 'An Un-
solved Historical Riddle.' There is no riddle about it
today: his career has been completely unriddled.[1]
Froude's follower in the Spanish archives, Martin
Hume, identified the speaking likeness of Pérez, the
'tawny knight of Spain', in *Love's Labour's Lost*.
Froude was on the right lines about Philip's Secretary
of State. Hitherto the sensational story had been told
in romances and dramas in terms of a triangular
love-story: Philip, Pérez and the insufferable Princess
of Eboli, ambitious, ugly, one-eyed. It was all politics,
which ordinary people rarely understand, and anyway
Pérez was a homosexual. They didn't know that either
(I don't suppose that Froude did: we progress, if only in
knowledge).

His portrait of St Teresa of Avila, illumined as it is
by his landscapes of Old Spain, shows how fair he
could be to a Catholic, even a Counter-Reformation,
saint. Once more we see him betwixt and between –
against the absurd idolatry accorded her by the credulous people, and the denigration of her by his fellow
Devonshireman, Richard Ford, of the famous Hand-
book to Spain. 'The idolatry may merit all that Mr
Ford has said about it, but the account which he has
given of the lady herself is so wide of the original . . .
the materials lie before him for a real portrait of
Teresa, had he cared to examine them.'

This Froude proceeded to give. 'It is the more
necessary since she has been deified into an idol, and
the tenderness, the humour, the truth and simplicity

1.   v. Gregorio Marañon, *Antonio Pérez*, and G. Ungerer, *A
Spaniard in Elizabethan England*, 2 vols.

of her human nature, have been lost in her diviner glories. . . . She was a Spaniard to the heart, generous, chivalrous, and brave.' What more could one want?

With his essay on 'The Templars' Froude ventured, as in several of his Short Studies, on a medieval subject. His account of the appalling brutalities with which the knights of the Temple were suppressed is corroborated by modern research – in any case his veracious portrayal is based on Michelet's *Procès des Templiers.* One knight, a de Villiers, deposed before the Pope's commissioners that he had seen his 'fifty–four brethren brought in carts and thrown into the flames.' Another was carried into court 'unable to stand: his feet had been held to the fire until they had been destroyed.' *Homo homini lupus.* Froude allowed that we need not assume that the persecutors 'did not believe in the Templars' guilt: men have a wonderful power of making themselves believe what they wish to believe'. As for the 'evidence' against them, the more one reads it 'the plainer it becomes that the confessions, and even the terms of them, were arranged beforehand'. The technique is not then merely modern, it goes back through the ages.

The foundation of this military Order went back to the Crusades, which Froude regarded, with some reason, as one of the supreme follies of the Middle Ages. The Templars were soldiers, and so they left no books, nothing in the way of literature; but they were 'famous for the beauty of their churches'. Froude was inspired by the Temple Church in London, and has a beautiful evocation of it, with the effigies of knights lying on the floor, 'almost in the condition in which they left it'. No longer: it has been destroyed by the fire-bombs of the barbarians of our time.

No doubt they too believed in what they were doing. Froude was right about humans.

Return to Oxford

Froude always loved Oxford. A quarter of a century or so after he had left it, he re-visited it, and wrote a nostalgic essay which he did not reprint in the four volumes of *Short Studies*. 'I felt that the happy allusion of Quevedo to the Tiber was not out of place here, "the fugitive is alone permanent". I saw things once familiar as I saw them before; but "the fathers, where were they?" I was in this respect like one awaked from the slumber of an age, who found himself a stranger in his own land. I walked through High Street. I entered All Souls and came out quickly, for the quadrangle or, rather, one glance around it, was sufficient to put "the past to pain." I could not deceive myself for a moment. There was an indescribable vacuum somewhere that indicated there was no mode of making the past the present.' For an old man re-visiting Oxford it is a place of ghosts.

All through his hard-working life in London Froude continued to write essays, and collected them in various volumes. As an historical essayist – not the same thing as being an historian – Froude is in the same class as Macaulay and Carlyle. He is not so high-spirited or such fun as the former, nor so original and incisive as the latter. He is more disparate, less concise and concentrated, but more varied. His essays range over the whole field of ancient, medieval and modern history.

Several of them make contributions to the history of the 19th century, particularly those on 'The Revival of Romanism', and 'The Oxford Counter-Reformation'. This formed a central issue of the time, particularly important for the Church of England; Froude was very close to it and well informed about it. He re-acted from an anti-clerical, layman's position, aware of the mystery of the cosmos but opposed to any dogma about it. His intellectual favourites were Spinoza, Lucian, Lucretius.

Two of the leaders of the Oxford Movement were 'distinctly men of real genius. My own brother was at starting the foremost of the party; the flame therefore burnt hot in my own immediate environment'. Then comes a significant historical reflection. 'We fancy that we are free agents. We are conscious of what we do; we are not conscious of the causes which make us do it; and therefore we imagine that the cause is in ourselves. The Oxford leaders believed that they were fighting against the spirit of the age. They were themselves most completely the creatures of their age.' A typical comment follows: 'My brother exaggerated the danger [from Benthamite Radicalism, Protestant Liberalism, etc], and underestimated the strength which existing institutions and customs possess so long as they are left undisturbed.'

In the 18th century scepticism had been fashionable, both in England and France. But 'the French Revolution had frightened all classes out of advanced ways of thinking, and society in town and country was Tory in politics, and determined to allow no innovations upon the inherited faith. It was orthodox without being theological. Doctrinal problems were little thought of.' Froude thought that a healthy state of affairs: his evidence is direct and to the point. The Oxford Movement divided the Church; it re-vitalised it on a narrower confessional basis; it had its influence throughout the English-speaking world; but in England it led directly to the revival of Romanism.

To Newman, 'if to any one man, the world owes the intellectual recovery of Romanism'. The famous controversy with Kingsley, which enabled Newman to explain himself to the world with his *Apologia,* took place 'on my account partly – at least, in reviewing a book which I had written'. Froude always retained an affectionate admiration for Newman. 'Greatly as his poetry had struck me, he was himself all that the poetry was, and something far beyond. . . . Newman's mind was world-wide. He was interested in everything which was going on in science, in politics, in literature.' He was not an ordinary person; his influence has become world-wide.

The argument of Newman's life and work was that God 'speaks to man and makes known his nature and his will' only through the Catholic Church – *securus judicat orbis terrarum.* If that is the case, Froude draws his own conclusion: 'then the attempt to understand this world, and what goes on in it, had better be abandoned in despair'.

In the following essay, on 'Origen and Celsus', Froude makes his own position clear, though he had to be careful in the Victorian age how he put it. 'Religion as a rule of life neither is, nor can be, a record of events which once occurred on a corner of this planet.' He agreed with Celsus, the pagan rationalist: 'his method of thought was scientific in the strictest modern sense; he disbelieved evidently that the order of nature was ever interrupted by supernatural interference' – as against the miraculous nonsense that Origen believed. On the other hand, Froude respected the practical good works that Christianity had achieved. It 'abolished the gladiator shows and the fights of men with wild beasts . . . forbade the strong to seize the helpless and make them slaves, or to expose children to die lest population should become redundant. The genius of Christianity has covered Europe with hospitals for the sick; has imposed on nations and duty of contending against plague and famine; has created a new virtue in *charity* which was unknown to Aristotle', etc. All this is an improvement on Gibbon.

When we come to the Middle Ages, in the essay on 'The Life and Times of Thomas Becket', Froude gives us a more convincing account of this remarkable man than Stubbs does, with his clerical bias. Froude's judgment is more in keeping with the modern view, sympathetic to Henry II who had a case for subjecting criminous clergy to the ordinary courts, instead of leaving them to the licensed liberty of the Church. The King was defeated by the martyrdom. 'Every superstitious mind in Christendom was at work immediately – generating supernatural evidence which should be universal and overwhelming. When once the impression was started that Becket's relics were working miracles it spread like an epidemic.' – This was the word for it.

Several of these essays are of the length of a short book. 'Annals of an English Abbey' illustrates, from the records of the sad state into which the great monastery of St Albans had fallen, the necessity of drastic reform or dissolution. The theme is dealt with generally in a Short Study on 'The Dissolution of the Monasteries'.

Essays on Elizabethan seamen expand into treatments of the Colonies: he devoted a book to his journey to the West Indies, (December 1887, immediately reprinted the following February). Ireland also gets the treatment, in 'Ireland since the Union', in which history merges into current politics. Froude never feared thus to engage himself, since he had no restricted academic view of history.

Nevertheless he would have liked to return to academic life, and stood several times for professorial chairs – to be passed over for people inferior to him: I suppose he was thought too 'controversial' by the conventional. He made it up with his old college, Exeter, when the Rector courteously invited him to replace his name on the books. In those days when chairs were not so common, it was something to be a Professor – though at All Souls they were traditionally regarded as second-class citizens. Froude's junior and enemy, Professor Freeman, 'went pop in Spain' – in Lytton Strachey's irreverent phrase – in 1892. To everyone's surprise Froude accepted the offer to succeed him as Regius Professor, though five years Freeman's senior and already nearly seventy-four.

I cannot think what made him accept this chore. He himself said, 'the temptation of going back to Oxford in a respectable way was too much for me. I must just do the best I can, and trust that I shall not be haunted by Freeman's ghost.' The assignment proved

more exhausting than he had expected; for, where no
one had attended the lectures of Stubbs and Freeman –

See, ladling butter from alternate tubs,
Stubbs butters Freeman, and Freeman butters
Stubbs –

everyone crowded to hear the famous old man, a
prodigal returned. Sir Charles Oman told me that it
was a 'golden age' of history lecturing in Oxford. After
Froude, again no-one attended the lectures of his
successor, Sir Charles Firth, as I remember.

Froude took too much upon himself; for, with such
réclame and finding himself the centre of so much
interest, he actually wrote out a course of lectures for
each term in which they were delivered. These were
then published in book form. *The Life and Letters of
Erasmus* is an important book. The best biography of
Erasmus today is Huizinga's; but as the foremost
Erasmus-scholar, P.S. Allen, wrote, Froude's book is
the best introduction, for one can read Erasmus' own
letters in it and they give one a veracious portrait of
the time by its most observant witness, its acutest
intellect.

I find the Ciceronian Latin which the Humanists
re-introduced hard to read – pity that medieval Latin,
geared to modern languages, ever went out. Froude
renders Erasmus readably into modern English for us –
naturally with occasional mistranslations, for he was
working swiftly as usual, and from an old Leyden
edition of 1702. One must always remember that 19th
century scholars had not the aids we have on every
hand. Froude tells us that, for the reader's benefit, he

was 'obliged to abridge, compress, and epitomise'; the reader should be correspondingly grateful, for it makes an admirable, living book.

Consistently with his practice all through, he recommends the reader to go to the original documents. Erasmus himself cautioned students against 'loading their memories with the errors of inferior writers'. This book gives one a portrait of Renaissance society, lit by its brilliant early hopes, then deluged by the dark flood of the Reformation. Erasmus and Luther (about whom Froude wrote a brochure in 1883) have a symbolic significance for him, the one representing the sceptical side, the other the activist. 'Goethe could say of Luther that he had thrown back for centuries the intelligence of mankind, by calling the passions of the mob to judge of matters which should have been left to the thinkers.'

Here I hold with the most enlightened of Germans, though regarding what happened as inevitable, as usual with common mankind. Froude not: he thought of the Reformation as a liberation of the spirit from the shackles of the medieval Church – to put it in less catholic and flexible shackles, one might say. This was rather democratic of Froude. An élitist like Burckhardt would opt differently: sufficient for the masses to be swaddled in the cocoon of some faith or other, so long as elect spirits are free – to think as only they are capable of thinking, to create in arts and sciences what they only are capable of creating: the real test of a civilisation.

Froude continued the story of the 16th century conflict to the threshold of the Counter-Reformation, with his *Lectures on the Council of Trent*. Since, as usual, Catholics and Protestants gave only their biased accounts, and since he was usually attacked for being merely pro-Protestant, 'I shall rely on Catholic documents of undoubted authenticity, on the testimony of Catholic witnesses antecedent to or contemporary with the Reformation.' Thus leading authorities for him were the letters of Cardinal Contarini (who was something of a reformer), and the History of Fra Paolo Sarpi (who was, however, anti-Papal).

The result was to do no justice to the difficulties of the Papacy, which could not have squared the circle, or bridged the gap, even it it had wished to. One cannot bridge a geological fault: the split was inevitable – that should obviate partisanship and taking sides, as people are only now, with ecumenicism, beginning to see. Froude held with the secular views of the Emperor Charles V, who was a devoted son of the Church equally anxious for Reform. When he proposed his middle-of-the-road Interim, the Protestants rejected it, while the Catholics would not consider it. They went on their separate ways, largely Northern Europe against South.

Believing in action, as one part of him did, Froude may not have recognised the impossibility of any Reform holding Christian Europe together. The Papacy did, and was content for the Council of Trent to reorganise the Church on the restricted basis of the Counter-Reformation. Hence the appalling Thirty Years' War in the next century.

With Froude's last lectures at Oxford, *English Seamen in the Sixteenth Century*, he returned to his earliest love. The effort exhausted him: no one could do, what he attempted – write a new course of lectures on a different subject every term. They were published posthumously by his surviving son,[1] who tells us that 'they were attended by all sorts and conditions of men and women, and had to be given in the New Schools for lack of space in the ordinary lecture room.' He also gives us the consoling thought that those last two years at Oxford 'were to him a return to a harbour from which he had been driven forty-five years before. Froude's literary life was not a summer cruise, but a long and arduous voyage through rocky and uncharted channels, rough seas, and adverse currents.'

He adds that Froude was 'at home in any type of boat, from a racing eight to a trawler; but, when sailing, was rather apt to take chances with his life and his gear.'

We may take that as an appropriate epigraph for his work.

He came back from Oxford that summer to die at Salcombe, within sight and sound of the estuary he had known so well and often sailed. Rather touchingly he wished to have the inscription on his tomb, 'Regius Professor of Modern History, Oxford.'

---

1. Ashley Froude gave me my copy, with an Oxford letter from his father.